YOU CAN'T STAY HERE

———

Sam Hedenberg

IDBH Media

YOU CAN'T STAY HERE

For Robert

CONTENTS

DISCLAIMER

A quick note:

While all of the stuff in this book absolutely happened, I've changed a lot of identifying details, including the purposeful omission of the brewery's name. This is to ensure the privacy of my co-workers and customers.

But I guess if you squint hard enough, you might see yourself.

INTRODUCTION

When you ask a kid what they want to be when they grow up, their response is pretty predictable: fireman, doctor, astronaut.

My dream was to become a writer or quarterback for the Philadelphia Eagles; two things that are still basically true today.

You know what job is never on that list? Bartender.

I started slinging suds for the same reason most do: necessity.

With our wedding approaching, my fiancée and I realized we couldn't cover our costs with just our day jobs. If I really wanted a steak option and an open bar, I needed another gig.

Aside from waiting tables during high school, I didn't have any experience in the service industry, but I figured the flexible hours and my love of beer made it a good fit.

I walked into the brewery one May afternoon planning to make some quick cash and bow out once the bills were paid.

What I didn't expect was that I'd fall head over heels for the job.

Five years later, I'm still behind the bar two or three days a week, pouring beers, talking shit, and grinning through whatever customer service situation gets thrown my way.

—

This book isn't a tell-all about the seedy underbelly of the bartending industry, nor is it a rant about bad customers. It's more a study in humanity, a series of observations that can only be collected from my vantage point behind the bar.

The thing about bartenders is that they're practically invisible. Think about the last time you sat down for a drink. Do you remember what

1

your bartender looked like? Their name, their hairstyle? Unless it was Tom Cruise flipping liquor bottles, I'm guessing not.

This anonymity, along with the tongue-loosening effects of alcohol, affords me the opportunity to see the parts of people they usually hide in public.

Behind the bar, I've witnessed marriages fall apart, babies being made, and grown adults shitting their pants. I've seen strangers become friends and friends become enemies. I've been treated like a king and a servant within a matter of minutes.

When I experience these things, I'm never disgusted or critical. It's actually quite the opposite. I'm fascinated and envious when people can be their true, ugly selves in public and not worry about who's watching. I'd never fall off a barstool and have the balls to do it again the next week.

What follows is my love letter to the best job I've ever had and the people I've served.

A CASE OF MISTAKEN IDENTITY

The first thing I learned about bartending at a brewery is that a quarter of customers don't understand where they are.

An older gentleman in a sharply-cut business suit walked in the door just after 5 one afternoon, his eyes trained on the ceiling rafters like an Alzheimer's patient.

Once he got his bearings, he approached the bar and asked for a menu. When I pointed to the chalkboard mounted on the wall, he sighed and squinted at it.

"Can you just tell me what red wines you have?"

This scenario plays out between four and 10 times a shift, and I have the unfortunate duty of explaining that, since we're a brewery, we only serve beer. No wine, no liquor. Just. Beer.

It's not totally their fault. Terms like "bar," "brewery," and "taproom" are often used interchangeably, even though they're not synonymous. Each category is governed by a different set of liquor laws, which varies state-by-state.

I never mind explaining the differences, and customers are usually good sports about it. But every once in awhile, they dig into me like I'm holding out on them.

"I don't like beer," a Lily Pulitzer-wearing mom spat at me last summer when I told her we didn't have chardonnay.

"Sounds like you came to the right place!" I said cheerily.

She was not amused. "What am I supposed to drink?"

"I have sodas if you'd like," I said.

She threw up her hands. "This is *unbelievable*. Just forget it."

3

I wondered which part she thought was so unbelievable, that a brewery served beer, or that I managed to refrain from reaching across the bar and putting her in a headlock.

—

Sometimes it takes a few tries for customers to understand exactly what's happening.

"I'll have a glass of merlot," one man requested during a Thursday happy hour. He was stately-looking, his gray hair swept to the side, his dress shirt open at the collar. He frowned when I told him we didn't have wine, but he didn't lose hope.

"A gin and tonic then," he said.

"I'm afraid we only serve beer," I said.

He grimaced like I'd just told him we only serve cat piss. "Fine," he said. "Just a soda water and lime."

Boy, this guy was really striking out. "I'm sorry, sir. We don't have those things here."

The blood in his cheeks creeped toward his tortoise-shell glasses. "What exactly DO you have here?" he asked.

"I have beer and soda."

"Do you have water?"

"I do."

"Great, a glass of ice water, then. PLEASE."

At this point it was all I could do to keep from giggling. "We don't have ice, but there's a filtered water station around the corner," I said.

From behind the bar, I can't see around the corner, but if I could, I'm sure I'd have witnessed hundreds of disappointed customers over the years discovering what I called a *filtered water station* is no more than a water fountain and a stack of Solo cups. I agree it's a stretch, but it's not like I'm lying. It's a station where you can get water, and I mean, I don't know how water fountains work, but there's GOT to be some kind of filter in there somewhere, right? At the least, it's better than what I can give them here, which is lukewarm sink water.

—

Our lack of ice is another sticking point for a lot of customers who like their beverages diluted beyond recognition.

Dear ice lover: I promise I'm telling the truth when I say there is not

4

a cube in the whole building. The only thing I have in the freezer are a couple of chemical first aid packs and a box of faux-chicken patties one of the bartenders eats for dinner.

This was hard to hear for one customer who liked his conversation cold and his beer colder.

"Gimme a cup of ice," he demanded.

When I gave my normal apology, his steely eyes bulged. "How do you NOT to have ice at a bar?" he asked.

"What do you need ice for?" I asked

"What do I NEED ice for? How about ICE COLD BEER?"

"It comes out of the taps at 38 degrees," I said. "How much colder do you need it?"

—

I understand you're disappointed we don't serve that glass of bourbon you dreamed about all day, but it ABSOLUTELY doesn't give you license to just bring it yourself.

On average, I confiscate contraband booze twice a month, most of which I find secreted in coffee cups and water bottles like the customers are drunk sophomores at homecoming.

Whenever I confront them, they feign surprise. "Oh my, I didn't realize," they'll say.

Really? I want to reply. *Do you also know it's bad form to bring a Big Mac to Benihana?*

I also get a lot of smugglers who tell me they brought their own drinks because they're allergic to gluten. And honestly, I'm really sorry about that. Unfortunately, you just walked into a literal gluten FACTORY on your own accord. If you're allergic to bees, I wouldn't recommend getting into the honey business either.

Still, our policy doesn't deter some.

Rick, a regular who comes three times a week with his girlfriend, called me over and told me his 84-year-old mother was visiting on Thursday, and they'd be coming to have dinner. The only problem was that Mom didn't drink beer. "Do you guys have a corking fee or anything?" he asked.

Rick pressed his lips together when he heard the bad news. "What if I just brought a little something for her, and you know..." He made a sneaky sipping motion.

"That would be against the law," I said. "Our license doesn't allow outside alcohol."

"But I mean, come on. It's my mother. She doesn't drink beer."

Sounds to me like you're bringing your mother to the wrong fucking place, Rick, I thought.

"It's not really my call," I said. "It's a LAW."

"I think it'll be fine if we just bring some in a little container," Rick's girlfriend said. "You know, just hide it."

"Ma'am, if the state decided to do a random inspection and found Mom sucking down smuggled chardonnay, we'd get shut down quicker than a pride parade in Alabama."

Rick's girlfriend gave me a conspiratorial nod. "It'll be our little secret."

"Of course," I said. "Just between us." Then I returned to the bar and snitched like Fredo Corleone.

I didn't work that Thursday, but I would've paid money to see the other bartenders snatch that little old lady's tumbler of rosé and dump it down the sink.

SELF-SERVICE

The business model of a brewery can be off-putting to some people. When it comes to customer service, we're basically a step above your buddy's man cave.

For some customers expecting a Michelin-star experience, this is confusing. For others, it's offensive.

I once served a woman who came in and asked if our kitchen was still open. She had short, gray hair, and her eyes darted in their sockets like a caged animal.

I told her we unfortunately didn't have a kitchen, but the food truck outside would be open until 8.

She wrinkled her nose. "You mean it's SELF-SERVICE?" she said.

"You don't have to cook the food yourself, if that's what you mean," I said. "They'll make it for you and hand it to you on a plate and everything. You will have to chew it yourself, though."

"If I want a beer, I can sit over there and you'll come take my order?" she asked.

I said no, customers order at the bar and then sit wherever they'd like.

She reluctantly ordered her dinner and her beer and was about 3/4 of the way through it when she approached the bar again.

"I'd like an ice water, please," she said.

Oh, poor honey. She wasn't going to be happy with this answer at all.

"We unfortunately don't have any ice, but there is a filtered water station around the corner," I said.

Fetching her own water was over the line. "You're ALL self-service? How awful!" She stormed out the door, so disgusted she didn't even finish her beer.

You can't please everybody, I guess.

THE CHAMELEON

When I was just out of college, I sold guitars on commission at a store in Maryland, and I worked with this guy named Charles.

Charles was always at the top of the sales ranker, and he got there with what I thought were some pretty skeezy tactics.

He'd do this thing where he pretended to be a football fan so he had common ground with customers.

One time at the beginning of the NFL season, I overheard him talking to someone about how his "favorite" team, the Indianapolis Colts, were going to do big things this year.

"My guy Peyton is going to come back strong from his injury," he said, "I can feel it."

I was so disgusted by this absurd ruse, I had to intervene.

"You know Peyton signed with the Broncos, right?" I said.

Charles shot me a look like I'd just cock blocked him with the hottest girl in the room. "No way," he said, clutching his chest. "When did that happen?"

"I don't know," I said. "Five months ago?"

—

At the time, that shit didn't sit well with me. It felt disingenuous, like Charles was compromising his values for the sake of a sale.

But when I started tending bar, I found myself employing some of those same tactics.

It started with subtle code switching, greeting one customer with a "sup, bro?" and the next with a "good afternoon, sir," depending on what I thought they'd respond to best.

After awhile, I abandoned all pretense.

One Saturday morning, the first customer of the day sat down and started talking to me about the Olympics. He was in his mid-60s and had a Fox News mustache and drank the first half of his beer in one long gulp.

Now, I haven't cared about the Olympics since I was, like, 8, but in the interest of being agreeable, I nodded along.

He told me the U.S. women's soccer team was playing that afternoon, and he was rooting for New Zealand.

"I can't stand all that kneeling stuff," he said. "It's just disrespectful to our country. I want them to lose so they'll shut their mouths."

His logic struck me as pretty flawed. Like, did he think if they lost a match they'd somehow realize the error of their ways and start draping themselves in the American flag?

But explaining that to a guy on his second beer at 12:30 in the afternoon seemed futile, so I gave him a non-committal "hmmmmm."

The man pointed to the TV. "Now, women's beach volleyball. That's a sport I can get behind," he said.

"How come?" I asked.

He raised his eyebrows. "For obvious reasons." We both looked at the TV, where the camera zoomed in on a girl picking her wedgie.

"Right," I said.

He said one of the Olympic teams had gotten disqualified because their uniform had shorts instead of bikini bottoms. "And that's just ridiculous to me," he said.

I started to agree that it shouldn't make a difference, but he cut me off.

"The bikini bottom is a part of the sport," he said.

"Oh!" I said. "You think they SHOULD have to wear bikini bottoms."

"Absolutely," he said. "It's equipment critical to the game."

"Makes sense to me!" I replied.

———

I know what you're thinking. How can I sleep at night knowing I've whored out my own values for the sake of money?

I still think my motives are more honorable than Charles's were. He was trying to grab cash, and all I really want to do is please people. But at the end of the day, Charles and I aren't all that different, are we?

We're chameleons, code-switching to fit in, to please, to get ahead.

Honestly, if it means my customers have a better experience, I'm happy to morph into an ultra-liberal or a womanizing bro for a few minutes.

There was one time when a guy and his friends came in for a bachelor party. He was pretty put together when they arrived, but by last call, his dress shirt was unbuttoned to his navel.

While waiting for their Uber, the groom said his wedding would be on August 7th, and I told him my wife and I were celebrating our fourth anniversary the day before.

His face brightened. "Respect, brother." He gave me a fist bump. "I mean, I've been married once before, but four times? That's incredible."

I thought about explaining his error, but I didn't want to disappoint him. He just seemed *so* impressed. Instead, I brought over a round of nightcaps.

The group raised their glasses. "What do we toast to?" one friend asked.

"To honor!" the groom said.

"To honor!" the group repeated. Then, in unison, they recited:

"If you can't come in her, come on her."

The group cheered and chugged their beers.

When their Uber arrived, I wished the groom luck on his wedding day.

"She's a special girl," he said, looking wistfully into the distance. "But, you know, life happens."

"What a lucky lady," I said.

WHERE EVERYBODY KNOWS YOUR NAME

During my time working at the brewery, I've served quite a few famous names. Michael Strahan, Joe Walsh, Chris Brown, Andy Reid, Jim Brewer, and Anne Hathaway have all graced my stools, and it's been a pleasure to serve them.

Of course, these weren't the *actual* celebrities. You think celebrities drink at my bar? No way. The most famous person I've ever served is a tie between the singer of a local ska band and a sports talk radio host who was recently fired for using a racial slur on the air.

Opening tabs for so many people makes you realize how cruel parents can be when naming their children. There's Crystal Ball, Misty Waters, and a customer whose tab shows up on the computer as MIGHTY TASTY BEAVER. One day I served Charles Brown, whom I immediately felt bad for. The Poor guy probably has someone yelling GOOD GRIEF at him twice a day.

Another older gentleman had the name Paul Running. "Like you're running away," he said.

"Good name," I said.

"it's a curse," he replied with a hint of disdain.

I could see his point. "Yeah," I said, "because you're walking somewhere, and everyone is like "what the hell is Paul doing?"

—

In an effort to provide excellent service, I do my best to remember customers' names. The creators of *Cheers* weren't wrong; we all want to go to a place where everybody knows our name.

The problem is that I'm absolutely TERRIBLE with names. When I'm introduced to someone at a party, I shake their hand and focus, but within 30 seconds, it's gone.

For the regulars I should know but am too embarrassed to ask, I'll just use a creative description in the computer. "Blue shirt by wall," or "Army hat." Even though it doesn't show up on their receipt, I always keep the descriptions objective out of fear they'll see I named their tab "creepy Bob Ross" or "Crypt-keeper."

—

Sometimes even if I do remember a customer's name, it backfires. One night, there were two large parties in the taproom, and ALL of their names were Rodriguez. The whole night, these 20 people would order beers, say "Rodriguez tab," and walk away.

"Look man," I said to one of them finally. "I've got like nine Rodriguez tabs, and I'm having a hell of a time keeping them all straight."

He said it wasn't a big deal because it happened to him all the time. "One time I was at a bar full of Spanish people, and the bartenders kept putting every Rodriguez drink on my tab," he said. "I ended up spending like $500."

I'd imagine the Smiths and Browns of the world have similar issues. Hedenbergs, though, not so much.

The customers aren't always so helpful.

"It looks like we have two Armstrong tabs right now," I said to one customer when he tried to close out. "What's your first name?"

"Mike," the man said.

I looked at the screen. "I don't have a Mike Armstrong. I have a Kurt and a James."

"James?" he said. "That's me, but nobody's called me James in years!"

"Except your bank, apparently," I said, pointing to his credit card.

"That doesn't count."

"It does when you open a tab with a card."

He chuckled. "Ah, I'm sorry man. It's just that Irish Catholic bullshit."

"I hear you," I said. "What's in a name, anyway? A rose by any other name would smell just as sweet."

"Exactly," Mike/James said. "It's bullshit."

—

The frustrating thing about all the effort I put into learning my customers' names is that most of them couldn't care less about mine. Not that it matters, I guess. I don't trust people who over-use names in conversation. It makes me feel like they're trying to sell me something.

"You know what I'm thinking, Sam, is that you could use someone to take a look at your current insurance rates. How'd you like that, Sam? You want to save some money?"

What's clear to me is most customers barely look at who's serving them. Jack, one of the other bartenders, is constantly being mistaken for me, despite bearing no resemblance to each other. A customer will start talking to him about being a teacher or how his new book is going or how the Phillies are doing.

Jack said he got tired of correcting people, so now he steers into the skid, making up wild details about my backstory. "I *was* a teacher," he'll say, "but after the investigation, they didn't think it was a good idea for me to be around kids anymore."

—

I think it's clear from all this confusion we'd be much better off overhauling the whole naming system. Mandatory name tags might help.

Once, during an Army/Navy football game, a group of vets threw a party in the taproom, and each of them wore a sticker containing not only their name, but also the team they were rooting for. Mary — Navy.

I think we can take this idea and run with it. If we all wore name tags like this, I'd have a much easier time navigating the world. LISA — VOTED FOR HILLARY AND STILL MAD ABOUT IT, or DON — HITS HIS KIDS, BUT ONLY WHEN THEY DESERVE IT.

At the very least, we should make names serve a more functional role, like they used to. Back in the day, Jim Miller was a miller, Mike Smith was a blacksmith. Wouldn't it be helpful to know your buddy Tommy Footfetish was a sick fuck? You'd sure never trust Kathy Looselips with a secret ever again.

—

Until these brilliant ideas can make their way into the legislature, I'll have to deal with the embarrassment of blanking when a familiar face stands before me.

Then again, my genius plans would prevent me from playing name games with customers, like I did late one Friday night.

A customer who'd been sitting there quite some time caught my attention as I passed his seat, and when I said hello to him, he smiled, showing a chipped front tooth that looked like a fang.

"You look like mffergsh," he said.

"I'm sorry?" I replied.

He repeated himself, but I still didn't hear him. I couldn't get that last word, either because of the loud music or his slurred speech, or both.

I never quite deciphered the word, even after I leaned over and put my ear inches from his mouth, but I got the gist he was commenting on what I was wearing, a plaid flannel shirt and beanie.

"Oh this?" I said. "It's part of my costume. It's the character I play. Hipster bartender."

"Your character?" he asked, his eyes swimming in their sockets.

"Yeah, exactly. It's for a role I'm researching. I'm an actor."

"Really?" he said.

"Absolutely."

"What movies have you been in?"

"Well…" For some reason, out of the countless movies I've seen in my lifetime, only one bubbled to the surface. "You ever see the movie *Fargo*?"

"Yes!" he said. "I love that movie!"

"There you go. I'm in *Fargo*."

His mouth opened and he tried to conceal a smile. "No way," he said, his jagged tooth there, in the middle of his face like a broken windowpane. "What part did you have?"

"You remember the guy in the woodchipper?"

"Of course!"

I cocked my thumb into my chest. "That was me."

"Seriously?"

"Dead serious." I said.

We were getting busy so I left the guy to serve other customers, but a few minutes later, he called me back over. He handed me a coaster. "I have to tell my friends I met you," he said. "Would you mind signing this for me?"

"Well, normally I don't do this," I said, "but I like you." I took a pen out of my pocket. "It's always nice to meet a fan."

I wanted to make sure whomever he showed this coaster to could read it, so I half signed, half printed the name STEVE BUSCEMI and handed it back to him.

"Oh, thank you so much," he said, examining the coaster. "I'm so excited."

"You're welcome," I said. "What's your name?"

He said something I couldn't make out, but it didn't matter. I stuck out my hand. "Great, I'm Steve. So nice to meet you."

JUST THE TIP

The crew of old men who come in every Thursday night was at it again this week, spreading their strange feast of pretzel bites and pepperoni slices across their table and promptly abandoning it to smoke cigarettes outside.

After they'd completed their weekly ritual of telling dirty jokes too loud and ripping through a pack of Marlboros, they came up to close out their tabs.

For Jimmy, the group's unofficial ringleader, this is a difficult task. Whenever I read him his total, he stares into his wallet and reaches in like it's a bucket of scorpions.

This week was no different. For his $21 tab, Jimmy thumbed through his cash, put a 20 and a 10 on the bar, then thought better of it and replaced the 10 with three ones.

"Alright there, Sam," he said. "You can keep that."

"Thanks Jimmy," I said, putting the extra $2 in the tip jar. "Great to see you."

"I'll get you better next week," he said.

I've served Jimmy every Thursday for five years, and every week, he promises a better tip next time. He's the customer equivalent of that cheesy sign hung up in bars that reads *FREE BEER…TOMORROW.*

—

As much as I love my job, the reason I'm standing behind the bar is to make money. And the majority of my pay comes from tips.

This can get tricky, because there are no hard and fast rules about gratuity. As such, the amount of money I make during any given shift can vary wildly. Some customers are incredibly generous; others skipped that chapter in Emily Post.

I've worked with several bartenders over the years who are obsessed with counting their tips. It's like they have a Terminator-style head-up display rolling figures and formulas across their vision, calculating exactly what they're making at any given moment. These are usually the bartenders who run over to examine a check the second a customer vacates their stool, rolling their eyes when they see the number on the dotted line. "Eighteen percent," they'll say. "Can you believe it?"

My feelings on collecting tips are contrary to these bean-counting bartenders. I tend to take the watched-pot-never-boils approach. I never get rattled when someone tips poorly, because I know it always comes out in the wash at the end of the night.

There are, of course, a few exceptions.

—

There's nothing worse than the guy who comes in with his co-workers and makes a show of putting his card down for the whole party. You know the type: striped shirt, slicked hair, shoes that look like something a Pilgrim would wear.

The untrained bartender gets excited about this dude dropping his Amex, thinking he's a high roller. But that's all part of his show. He'll grab each colleague around the shoulders and escort them to the bar. "Order anything you want," he'll say, as if there is anything on the menu other than $7 beers. And then he'll turn to me and say "make sure this goes on MY tab."

Nine times out of 10, when closing out, this guy will look at his bill, check over his shoulder to see if anyone's watching, and fill in a tip around eight percent. To his co-workers he's the hero, but I know the real story.

Crusty old men never tip well either. I'm not sure if it's because they're mad at the world and taking it out on me, or if they're stuck in the '70s. These guys tip a dollar — or in some cases, 50 cents — for each drink, which would be incredible if beers were still $3 a pint.

These are the same people incredulous about the price of milk or so out of it they think you can still catch a matinee and a bucket of popcorn for under 10 bucks.

One guy I served for years would tip me $3 every time he visited, regardless of whether his tab was $7 or $70.

I had another customer who tipped much better, but he always gave it to me in $2 bills.

"Why do you have so many $2 bills?" I finally asked him. "Do you make a special trip to the bank to get these, or did your grandma just send you a card for your birthday?"

—

I don't want to get preachy. I absolutely believe what your server or bartender deserves is at your discretion, and I'm not so petty that what you tip me affects your level of service.

That said, people who compensate the bartenders well ARE remembered when they come through the door. Once, on a slammed Friday night, I saw a customer who always tipped north of 30 percent unable to find a place to sit with his wife. I pulled out an extra table from the back and waved him over to it. It was some real *Goodfellas* shit I wouldn't have done for just anyone.

Whatever you decide to tip, for the love of god, resist the urge to write MATH on the tip line and make me figure it out. I know it seems cute and clever, but allowing me to do the arithmetic on your tip assumes I have more prowess in adding and subtracting than you do, which I assure you I do not. I'm counting that shit on my fingers like a second grader, so don't get mad at me if I enter the wrong amount.

—

When someone stiffs me on a tip, the truth is I'm not mad at them. It's more that I'm embarrassed for them. I want to explain how the exchange of an appropriate amount of currency is not about greedily lining my pockets with their hard-earned cash, but about extending a symbolic gesture of decency and respect. I'd love to pull Jimmy close and tell him what's happening; not to scold him, but to guide him toward being a better human.

But tipping is an unspoken agreement between server and servee, so I smile and wave goodbye and try to believe when he says he'll get me next time, he really means it.

FRIENDS AND FAMILY

If you're ever feeling lonely or like you don't have any friends, all you need to do is open a bar.

People you haven't heard from in years suddenly show up. Your kindergarten classmate, your accountant, the guy from Jiffy Lube who changed your oil in 2006. It's like owning a pick-up truck; most of the year, you're forgotten, but when it's time to move, you're more popular than Mark Hammill at a *Star Wars* convention.

The first two years I worked at the brewery, I'd get a customer every few days who'd ask for the owner. "Is Gene around?" they'd say, craning their necks to try and spot him in the back. "I was his roommate at the Academy."

At first I thought it was nice, an old Navy buddy stopping in to say hello, but once the number of patrons claiming to be Gene's roommate grew into the 30s, I became dubious.

"Gene sure did have a lot of roommates," I said to one supposed cohabiter. "Did you guys have bunk beds?"

—

I'm not certain of every name-dropper's motives, but I can only assume most of them are fishing for a discount.

I'm fascinated by people who ask for discounts, because it's something I'd never dream of doing myself. I don't have the courage to look someone in the eye and say *listen, I see your prices are posted right there, and I understand you've probably done some significant legwork to arrive at that product's value, but is there any possible way for me to pay less?*

My grandfather was the type of person who was never willing to accept the sticker price. He'd dicker over bills at restaurants, retail stores, service centers. I once even heard him ask for a discount on his electric bill. "My bill was almost $40 less last month," he said. "Is there any way you can make this lower?"

It seems my grandfather was not alone in these types of requests, but rather a member of a fairly large segment of the population.

"Go ahead and make the price as low as you can," a bar customer once said to me while I closed out his tab.

What I don't understand is the motive behind this compulsion. Are you really that concerned about the 35 cents I'm going to take off your beer by flashing a military ID? Or is it more for the sense of satisfaction, that feeling you've somehow won by paying slightly less than the sucker standing next to you?

Perhaps it's the sensation of exclusivity, the excitement of executing the secret handshake that gets you behind the velvet ropes. And I totally understand that desire. Aside from my son being born, the most joyous moment of my life was walking into In & Out Burger for the first time, touching the side of my nose and saying "and an order of fries. *Animal style.*"

The problem comes in the execution, when customers ham-handedly fumble through a transparent attempt to gain access to the inner sanctum.

Once, a dude I didn't recognize came up and ordered a beer, and I handed it to him and asked him if he had a tab.

He pointed to a table of regulars. "I'm with Scott and Jeff over there."

"So I should put it on Scott's tab?" I replied.

He fumbled for a response, which I expected. He thought saying Scott's name was some kind of password that would grant him free beer, and that was not how it worked. "I think Scott has a tab, yeah," he finally got out.

"Excellent. Scott's such a nice guy to buy your beers."

———

What's worse is when people don't understand that as the bartender, I am the gatekeeper to Discount Land. I spend my weekends scrubbing toilets and mopping floors and lugging kegs so I can wield the power of granting a menial discount to the people I find worthy. Why in god's name would you take that joy away from me by ASKING for it?

One Saturday afternoon, a girl told me she was friends with Todd, our market rep. Normally, I'd be like *cool, so am I,* but Todd had called ahead and asked us to take care of her, so of course I was going to.

But then this chick had the balls to break the cardinal rule.

"So like, do I get a discount or something?"

Likewise, I once served a customer who set two six packs on the counter and handed me his credit card. "Go ahead and throw the friends and family discount on there for me also," he said.

Our friends and family discount is 10 percent, which like, I get a better discount with coupons at Bed Bath and Beyond. So I wasn't about to argue with this dude about whether he was or was not eligible. I decided I was going to give it to him, but not before making him the object of my enjoyment.

I squinted and made a show of surveying his face. "Are you a friend or family?" I said.

"I'm friends with Rich," he said. Of course he was. Rich has been a brewer for as long as I've been there, and he's always got skeezy friends hanging around.

"Rich?" I said.

"Rich, the guy who works here," Friend said.

"Sorry man," I said, "there's nobody named Rich here."

Friend gave me the smug *you must be new here* face and pointed to Vinny, the other bartender. "Ask him about Rich."

I tapped Vinny on the shoulder, taking a gamble.

"Yo, you know a dude named Rich that works here?" I said.

Vinny thought for a second. "Not that I know of," he said, and he kept working.

Now Friend was getting confused. "Did he quit or something? He's worked here forever! He's a brewer!"

"A brewer?" I said. "You mean Clint? Will? Jeff? Those are our brewers."

"No, Rich," Friend repeated. "He's a brewer here, I swear!"

I apologized again. "Look man, I'm happy to give you the discount, but you might want to hit up your boy Rich and ask him why he's fucking with you. Because he definitely doesn't work here."

I handed Friend his receipt and waited on another customer. He stood there dumbfounded for a moment, and tried one last time to figure out if he was losing his mind.

"Yo dude," he said to the bar back. "You know the guy Rich who works here? He's a brewer."

"I'm sorry man, I only work here one or two days a week," the bar back said, whisking by him to pick up a pair of empty glasses.

—

While our military and friends & family discount are more or less public knowledge, there's yet another level of discount known only to insiders: the industry discount.

Even though I've been a bartender for five years now, the exact rules of the industry discount are still a little slippery to me. The gist, though, is if you're also a bartender or server, you get hooked up. The level of discount varies wildly: sometimes it's a percentage off your bill; sometimes you have a round or two comped; other times, your tab goes in the trash and everything's on the house.

In return, it's good form to leave a ridiculous tip, usually equal or greater to what your tab would have been without the discount. I'm not good at math, so I like going with tips in $10 increments.

The key to the industry discount is never to expect it. If I'm visiting another brewery, my move is to casually mention my place of employment, ask some questions, and bond with my brethren about toiling in the trenches of flights and stupid questions and feral children. I'll even bring in a six-pack from my brewery as a gift if I remember to.

Sometimes it works and sometimes it doesn't, but since I always tip more than what I would've paid anyway, it's less about saving money and more about fostering goodwill and leaving with the satisfaction of bonding with my fellow slingers of suds.

Of course, there are dickheads out there who can't get this right either.

Not long ago, a customer asked me to close his $24 tab, and as he started to sign the receipt, he looked up at me.

"Do you guys do an industry discount?"

Oh come on, dude. First off, the first rule of industry Fight Club is abundantly clear. Second, you're asking for a discount AFTER you close your tab? That's so fucking tacky.

In situations like this, I never outright say no. You want to morph into a douche dispenser to save the cost of a Red Bull? Go for it, super chief. Hope it was worth it.

I hit the ol' friends & family button for him, but not before messing with him a little bit.

"Industry discount?" I asked. "What industry?"

He pointed to his shirt, emblazoned with the name of some brewery I'd never heard of.

"You just walk around wearing the shirt of the brewery where you work?" I asked.

"Sure, why not?"

"I dunno man. That's like working at Target and rocking a red vest everywhere."

I refunded his $2.40 and handed him his new receipt. "There you go, homie. Next time at least bring me a sticker or something."

He left a $3 tip, like a real industry pro. Cool, dude.

For awhile, we had this really annoying girl who'd come in weekly, and since she worked at a brewery down the street, she mostly drank for free. We never *liked* hooking her up because she was a pain in the ass, but we honored the industry code.

Then we heard she got fired after having a falling out with the owner, and there was no greater pleasure than seeing her face when I handed her the tab the next time she came in.

"What's this?" she asked.

"Your bill?" I said.

"But I don't pay. I'm *industry*."

I explained that typically once you are no longer employed by the industry, you can no longer claim to be industry.

"I AM still employed by the industry. I'm a hostess at Ruby Tuesday's."

The punchline here should be self-evident, but it wasn't for this girl. I didn't have the heart to tell her Ruby Tuesday's was no more part of the beer industry than Wal Mart, so I compromised by giving her the friends & family discount. She saved $4.

—

The trick to maintaining your sanity at a bar is not letting every buttplug and weasel who comes through the door get to you. If I got wrapped around the axle every time some undeserving dunce shamed me into discount, I'd need a Lexapro prescription.

Instead, I focus on the good ones, the guys with the compelling story, the well-timed laugh, and the kind face. You could be the loneliest guy in the world, but if you take care of your bartenders, they might slide that door open and let you into the secret club with a "hey man, this one's on me."

THE WEEDS

It was the first nice day in September, and I was looking forward to the cooler temps attracting the customers who'd been hibernating in their air-conditioned houses all summer.

I could tell we'd be dead by the emptiness of the parking lot when I pulled in, and we were. I spent the night shifting my weight on the bar's concrete floor, watching episodes of *Family Guy*.

Forget waterboarding; if the CIA really wanted to torture terrorists, it should make them stand behind an empty bar for a night.

I know some people would love a job where all they had to do was kill the clock watching Netflix, but I much prefer being busy.

When the bar fills up, a zen overtakes me. My movements become more fluid, my senses sharper. Even my jokes get funnier.

My co-worker becomes my doubles partner, and we dance around each other with a grace that belongs on the court at Wimbledon. It is by far the most fulfilling part of the job.

But with every new customer that comes in the door, the taproom fills, and that carefree confidence I had is replaced with dread. Suddenly it feels like the whole building is going to collapse.

Welcome to the weeds.

—   .

The weeds is what bartenders call it when we can't keep up with customer demand. A line appears, and suddenly the hurry up theme from *Super Mario Bros.* plays on a loop in my head. The crowd that was once my source of energy is now a horde of charging savages hurling orders. If you've ever been at a busy bar and your server looks like he's being chased by a bear, you've seen him in the weeds.

Being weeded is the worst not just because my only thought for hours is *shit shit shit*, but because I start staggering around like a newborn foal.

I break stuff, too. One time when I was in the weeds, I dropped a glass, and by the time I reached out to catch it, it had already hit the ground and shattered. The shrapnel bounced into my outstretched hand, cutting me so deeply I soaked through a bar rag within 30 seconds.

I probably should've gotten stitches, but there were too many thirsty customers. I butterflied the wound shut with some Band Aids and got back on the floor.

Not to be outdone, the other bartender dropped an entire tray of glassware an hour later. She didn't get hurt, but she did draw a round of sarcastic cheers from the crowded bar.

The only thing you can do when you find yourself waist deep is to breathe and keep moving. I remind myself that eventually, the clock will strike last call, the crowds will thin, and it will be over.

FENG SHUI

My wife Melinda has this habit of perpetually re-arranging things in our house. I'll come downstairs to pour myself some coffee, only to find the cabinet that yesterday housed our cups is now full of spices.

When I ask what happened to the coffee cups, she makes an annoyed noise in the back of her throat and throws open the cupboard where the flour and sugar used to live. "They're right here, *obviously*," Melinda says, as though I'm a dementia patient and she's my caregiver, tired of fishing my slippers out of the toilet.

It's not just the pantry she's constantly revising, either. In our old house, there was a two-year stretch where I'd come home to a entirely new floor plan every couple of weeks. Couches would be in different rooms, the TV on a new wall, a bookshelf I'd never seen before occupying the space where my desk sat a mere eight hours prior.

The main reason I'm annoyed when I come home to a new living room is because when I'm working at the brewery, I am constantly battling a sizable percentage of customers who take it upon themselves to feng shui the taproom's furniture.

"Do you mind if we push these tables together?" one woman asked me on a busy Thursday afternoon. She pointed to two round hightops: one in the middle of the floor, the other in the corner across the room.

"Yeah, I do, sorry," I said.

"Okay, great, because — wait. We CAN'T push the tables together?"

I didn't make a friend by denying her request, but I appreciated that she at least asked. Some don't, and then I have the uncomfortable task of approaching them and explaining the table they just annexed to hold their three pizzas needed to be left where it was.

Whether asking permission or plowing ahead like they own the place, the next word out of the customers' mouths is always the same:

"Why?"

Is there any answer to that question that will truly satisfy you? Are you a toddler, trying to make sense of the world for the first time, or a reincarnated philosopher seeking meaning from life's largest table-layout mysteries?

Listen, I'd be lying if I said I rolled out a blueprint and placed tables like Eisenhower positioning troops but when I set up the bar, the tables are where they are for a reason. Customers shouldn't have to navigate a labyrinth of your bullshit tables to order a beer.

Of course I never say any of that. Instead, I go with the oldest chop from the service phrasebook: "sorry, my manager doesn't let us move the tables."

—

I know you think you're smarter than me because I'm standing on this side of the bar and you're on that side. But unless you're Joanna Gaines, I'm not going to give in.

You hear that, guy who wants to prop the front door open with a barstool so we can "get more airflow in here?" Or lady who scours the floor for empty seats and hoards 25 around your table that's designed for 10?

For whatever reason, our patio is the area that most stokes my customers' decoration desires. I think it's because they feel unsupervised, but I have very clear sight lines from my place behind the bar and have to witness the whole nasty process.

Once I interrupted a guy in flip flops and a tank top who was pushing all the tables to one side of the patio. I stood there for a minute, but when they failed to notice me, I cleared my throat and asked if everything was okay.

"Oh, yeah, we just want to play corn hole," Tank Top said. "You guys have corn hole boards, right?"

"We do, but they're not set up today," I said. "We set up these tables instead, as you can see."

"Oh," Tank Top said. "Can you go get the boards for us?"

The umbrellas we put over the tables in the summer are another issue. I've never seen so many umbrella tinkerers in my life. They crank it down, crank it up, wiggle the base, adjust the angle. So many people handle them every day, the umbrellas end up in tatters by the end of the season. Then, when they break, I have to feign surprise. *Really?* I want to say. *The base just fell apart? I'm sure it has nothing to do with your two kids spinning it like a pinwheel for the last hour.*

——

I guess there are times when I'm willing to make exceptions. I have a couple of customers who come with their own camping chairs so they can smoke cigars and not bother anyone. While I've never personally brought my own furniture to an establishment, I can see it's a mutually beneficial decision.

Where I draw the line is the guy who tried to set up his own canopy tent.

On a Thursday night, my partner Jack and I caught sight of someone with a tape measure taking notes about the size of our patio. Afterward, he approached the bar and explained he and his wife were coming on Saturday with their infant son, and they wanted some shade. So they planned on bringing their own canopy tent, and he wanted to make sure it was going to fit.

"That's cool, right?" he said.

Jack was diplomatic, but explained there was no way in hell he was going to be able to put up his own tent.

"Really? Why not?"

"Because if YOU bring a canopy, someone else sees it and brings THEIR canopy, and then a customer complains because one person's canopy is touching their canopy, and they're taking up too much space, and suddenly I'm not pouring beers because I'm negotiating pop-up tent turf wars on the patio."

As the customer walked away dejected, Jack turned to me. "How can you keep a straight face through a conversation like that?" he asked.

"I get lots of practice at home," I said.

ON DEAF EARS

I served a group of deaf people this afternoon. They're wonderful and polite, and while I know very little about ASL, it's fascinating to watch them talk to each other.

I think the biggest reason I wouldn't want to be deaf is because there's no such thing as a private conversation. Like, how do you whisper to someone? All of your communication is right out there for everyone to see. That would be tough for me, considering how much I like to talk shit under my breath.

While I did my best to be accommodating, my manager, Mark, had a different approach.

"You see those kids?" he said, pointing to the deaf group. "One of them was standing outside the chains, so I went over and told him to get back on the other side because he was breaking the law. And they all just stared at me, so I started yelling at them."

"How'd that go?" I asked.

"They just kept staring at me, and I was like 'what the fuck? Why are you ignoring me?' And then I realized —"

"Those customers are deaf," I said.

"They're fuckin' deaf! And I was yelling at them like an asshole!"

OFF THE HOOK

As anyone who's ever worked in the service industry will tell you, most of my job consists of spinning plates. If you want to avoid getting in the weeds, you have to understand how to multitask and how to prioritize.

Most things on the list are obvious: take care of the customers, clean the tables, stuff like that. And then way at the bottom — between refilling the toilet paper and staring at the wall — is answering the phone.

—

I really don't understand people who call us and expect someone to answer, especially if it's the weekend. The only person I know who calls a bar is Bart Simpson, and he's not real.

Actually, if Bart Simpson did call, at least it would be funny. The people who call the brewery are just sad and confused.

90 percent of the time, I get the same three questions:

1 - Do you have food? (No, but we have a food truck).

2 - What is your food truck tonight? (The same one we had LAST Saturday when you called).

3 - Are you pet friendly? (Unfortunately, yes).

These would all be valid questions I wouldn't mind answering if they all weren't in plain English on our website and social media accounts. You see that Google page where you found my phone number? Look three inches to the left. Those are our operating hours.

I don't buy the age of the caller as an excuse. You don't have any trouble reading the Drudge Report every morning, my guy, and I doubt you found my phone number in the Yellow Pages.

To be fair, part of my problem is a personal bias against telephones. No one was happier than me when restaurants started offering online ordering options, because it meant I never had to interact with another human to get takeout ever again. On more than one occasion, I've chosen a different pizza shop because they only took orders over the phone. The only person I talk to with any frequency is my mother, so I can hear about what doctors' appointments she and my father have scheduled for the upcoming week.

—

The silliest question I get frequently is from customers both young and old.

"Hi," said a girl who sounded young enough to be one of my high school students. "I was wondering how busy you are right now?"

For all the years I've worked at the bar, I've never figured out how to answer this question. Most of the time, we live somewhere between dead and slammed. What am I supposed to do, count the open stools and report back?

I wanted to tell the girl that my assessment of our capacity was about as useful as a TV traffic report, but instead, I pretended to scan the crowd and reply "um, medium busy?"

There was a long pause. "So do you think we'll be able to get a table?"

I'll usually say I think so or it shouldn't be a problem, but on this particular day, my patience had been worn down by a pair of girlfriends who'd wanted to sample every beer we had on tap. I was in no mood to placate.

"If you can get here in the next 30 seconds, the answer is yes," I said. "But beyond that, you're asking me to see into the future, and I unfortunately left my crystal ball at home today."

—

By far the strangest call I ever answered came on a Friday night while we were winding down. The dinner rush crowd started to close their tabs, and I was stacking stools on the patio when the phone rang.

"Can you guys play some R&B or rock music or something?" the caller asked.

I had no clue what this guy was talking about. "You mean do we have live music?" I asked.

"No, I mean on the stereo," he said. "I'm tired of this rave shit."

"We do sometimes," I said. "The music changes all the time."

"No," he said, "I'm saying can you change it right now."

The guy explained he was currently at the brewery with his buddies and dissatisfied with the music in the back room. I peeked through the window, and sure enough there he was, talking into his phone 100 feet away.

"I'll see what I can do," I said through gritted teeth.

I relayed the situation to Kristen, the other bartender, who suggested I turn on something more annoying, like death metal. But I'm not that spiteful. I just killed the music altogether. Problem solved.

When the guys came up to get another round, I realized they were regulars, and I knew them well enough to break their balls.

"You motherfuckers were too lazy to ask me to change the music?" I said. "You had to CALL ME?"

They laughed, and I plowed forward. "You're lucky I answered at all. I should've let it go to voicemail and let my manager deal with that nonsense in the morning."

They apologized for their sloth and left me a $20 tip for my trouble. I guess sometimes it's worth picking up the phone.

CHANNEL SURFERS

The employee handbook at the brewery isn't very long. A generous estimate is eight pages. We're a pretty small operation, and management isn't the type to go Avril Lavigne and make things complicated.

One thing it does clearly specify is we are to have sports playing on the taproom televisions at all times. I never understood why that's important enough to be printed in the handbook, but I follow it. I talk a big game, but I'm a rule follower at heart.

The problem with this policy are the conflicts it causes among our sportsfan customers. No matter what game I put on, it's inevitably the wrong one.

I can't think of a single time I've walked into a bar and asked them to change the channel, but this is something people apparently do. A lot.

One night during hockey playoffs, a customer asked me to change the channel so he could watch baseball. He had one of those sculpted beards that indicate he's given more than a few one star reviews on Yelp.

The mere act of me raising the remote toward the TV drew a chorus of boos from a table of dudes wearing Capitals jerseys.

"Sorry man, they're watching this," I said.

"Oh come on," Beard Guy said. "Hockey is so boring."

"Totally," I said. "I'm sure most people would agree playoff hockey is more boring than an inter-league baseball game in April, but they were here first."

—

The primary thing working against me is that we've only got two TVs and a basic cable package straight out of 1985. Some guys mistake our bar for a Buffalo Wild Wings and can't understand we only get six sports channels.

This happens the most during college football season, when there are 4,000 games being televised simultaneously on 4,000 obscure networks.

"Could you put on the Bucknell game? They're playing Colgate," a customer asked me one Saturday.

"What channel is it on?" I said.

He named some ESPN offshoot I'd never heard of on channel 3205.

I apologized and told him we only get regular ESPN, which was currently playing a game between colleges that weren't named after a fucking toothpaste.

"Would you mind checking anyway?" he asked. So, instead of pouring beers for other waiting customers, I stood in the middle of the room with a remote pointed to the heavens, clicking to channel 3205 and showing him we were not, in fact, subscribed to whatever the hell he was looking for.

It's only slightly better during the NFL season. Most customers are fans of the local Washington team — whatever their name is when you read this — but since DC is a transplant city, we get a lot of out-of-market requests. And it's my sad duty to inform these customers dressed in Bengals or Rams or Cardinals jerseys that they cannot watch their favorite team.

For awhile, we got this string of strange phone calls on Sunday mornings. The callers were all different people, but their question was the same:

"Are you guys showing the Bills' game today?"

We tried to understand for months why so many people had such a specific request. Were Bills fans so hard up to watch the game they were calling every bar in the phone book?

As the season wound down and the calls kept coming, I finally asked one caller why he thought we would be showing the Bills' game.

He said a fan site tracks Bills bars in every city, and our brewery was on the list.

"To my knowledge, we've never shown a single Buffalo game since I started," I told him. "But I appreciate your fire."

—

Our general policy on the TVs is first come, first served. But there are moments when common sense must prevail.

When March Madness happened last year, it was a big deal. The previous tournament had been canceled due to COVID, and sports betting had recently been legalized in Virginia. People were excited to get back to their brackets and maybe make a little cash.

On my first shift of the tournament, I tried to get ahead of requests by writing out a list of all the games. The first one came as soon as we opened from a regular named Roy, who comes in with his wife every Saturday.

"Is anyone watching that?" he asked, pointing to the NCAA pregame.

I readied my handwritten list. "Not really. I can put it on whatever game you want. There's Georgetown versus —"

"Can you put on golf?"

"Golf?"

"Yeah, like the Golf Channel?"

I wanted to make Roy happy, but also...who the fuck wants to watch day three of the Safeway Open during March Madness?

The rest of the customers didn't seem to mind, but as soon as Roy and his wife headed for the door, I changed the channel back to basketball by the time it swung shut.

I just wish people could read the room so I didn't have to be the bad guy all the time.

During the final round of this year's Masters Tournament, I had a bar full of dudes in fluorescent polos and Titleist hats watching the PGA's best battle for the green jacket. Three men approached the bar and didn't even order a beer before asking to put on a soccer game between Moldova and Estonia.

"Those countries have soccer teams?" I said. "I didn't even know they had running water."

"It's a HUGE game," one man said. His two friends nodded.

"Look, normally I'd say no problem, but look around. These dudes would have my head if I tried to turn off the Masters."

I got a few complaints, but I managed to avoid a full-on golf riot with a couple of comped beers.

In case you were wondering, Estonia vs. Moldova ended up tying 0-0, which is the reason soccer is the worst fucking game in existence.

There, I said it.

—

I generally don't care what's on TV because I'm too busy to watch anyway. But occasionally, when there's a Philly team in prime time, I'll put it on.

One year, the Phillies were one game out of first place, and I was happy to see them playing the Mets on ESPN. It was tied at the bottom of the third when a guy at the bar motioned me over.

"Can you put the Orioles game on?" he asked.

"The fucking O's?!" I said.

"They're playing Boston."

"The Phils are battling for the division," I said. "That hasn't happened in a decade!"

"Yeah, but I don't care about the Phillies," he said.

Where I'm from, that sort of talk would get you tossed out on your ass, but I'm not in Philly anymore, and I have to respect the hometown fans.

I reluctantly reached for the remote and flipped the channel, where the Red Sox were pummeling the Orioles.

"It's 7-0 at the top of the 8th," I said. "You really want to watch this garbage?"

"What can I say, I'm a masochist," the guy said. "It comes with being an O's fan."

Being in the service industry has taught me to be at the mercy of the customer, even if it means risking an angry horde of golfers or searching for a channel I know I don't have.

So I shut up and followed the Phillies clinch the division on my phone, letting the customer enjoy his beer with a side of Orioles defeat.

BAR ROMANCE

"You see those two over there?" my co-worker Rose whispered, pointing to a couple at a high top. "They're on a Tinder date."

"How do you know?" I asked.

"They did this greeting where he went in for the hug and she stuck out her hand," she said. "That kind of awkwardness only comes from a Tinder date."

The pair's interactions were the source of our entertainment the rest of the night, Rose providing the dialogue to their body language. When I cleaned the table next to them, I overheard the guy telling the girl about his boss.

"This woman is 36 years old, and she's never had her first kiss," he said. "And it sounds so weird to say, but her boobs are literally larger than your head."

So yeah, I'd say the date went well.

—

Watching couples interact is one of my favorite past times while I'm at work. It's fascinating what people see as appropriate demonstrations of affection.

Like the regular who always sits on the same side as his wife and plays with her hair the whole time. They have a couple of drinks and pay, and while they wait for their Uber, they make out like 8th graders, sometimes with her sitting on his lap.

One time, the guy made the shocker sign and thrust it at his wife. When he saw me watching, he grinned and wriggled his pinky finger. You know, the one that goes in the butt.

That same night, he grabbed his wife's boob and shook it like a magic 8 ball, and again, he caught me staring. "What?" he said. "I can't give my wife some love?"

Occasionally, couples get so enamored with each other, they can't even wait to get home before sharing their passion.

One night after we closed, I walked into the women's room to find two sets of feet facing the same direction in the handicap stall.

I closed the door quietly and left the pair alone. Who was I to interrupt such a beautiful moment?

The dude slunk out the front door a few minutes later, and 30 seconds after that, the girl followed. Smooth.

Vinny, the other bartender, cleaned the bathrooms afterwards, and I asked if there was any evidence of the liaison. "Did it smell like sour milk in there?" I asked. "Or Taco Bell?"

He said the baby changing table was folded down, which was confirmation enough for me.

"I have so many questions," Vinny said. "Like is this a first date, or have they been together for awhile? Why the stall? Why not the car?"

"These are all great questions that deserved answers," I said. "We really should have pulled them aside for a post-game interview."

———

Of course, for every pair of lap-sitters and bathroom fornicators, there are a dozen who act normally. One of my favorite couples, Ben and Ashley, visit two or three times a week and play cards. They're always good for a friendly chat and a couple of jokes.

I like watching them because they're so at ease and enjoy each other's company, which is why I was so distraught when Ben came in with his side chick.

Part of my job is to be discreet about things like that, I guess. But I was surprised and a little disappointed. C'mon Ben, playing pinochle with your mistress at the same high top where you had your wife two days before? That's low, man.

I wanted to see what this home wrecker looked like, so I made an excuse to walk past their table and retrieve empty glasses.

It wasn't some hussy, though. It was his Ashley, fresh from the salon with a new hairstyle.

I was so relieved I went over and explained to them what I thought was happened, and they laughed.

"It's good to know you've got my back," Ashley said.

—

And for the most part, I do have my customers' backs. When you spend so many nights waiting on people, you begin to form a bond with them. Not a friendship, per se, but a relationship that extends beyond an exchange of goods and money.

If you stick around a place long enough, you see love sprout, like the couple who met at the bar and eventually held their wedding reception there.

Sometimes you see it die. A guy I served several times a week would bring in his wife and kids. He never stopped coming, but the wife and kids disappeared, and eventually they were replaced by a new woman. It was clear who got the bar in the divorce.

I never brought it up with him because I didn't want things to get awkward, like it did with Carrie.

"Where's Colin tonight?" I asked, trying to make conversation.

She made a little hitching noise and then melted into puddles on the bar. "We…broke…up," she sobbed.

She told me the whole sordid story, how he was afraid of commitment and she felt like she deserved more.

There's a kernel of truth to the whole bartender-as-therapist trope. I didn't polish a glass while I consoled Carrie, but I did listen to her, and when she was done, I offered my advice.

"Fuck that guy," I said, putting another drink in front of her. "You're better off without him."

She straightened and wiped her nose with the back of her hand. "You're right," she said. "Fuck Colin. I don't need him."

She finished her drink in one long gulp and wobbled out into the night, buoyed by my dime store philosophizing.

I didn't see Carrie again for another month, when the door swung open and she was there.

I greeted her and in my head began spinning up some cliched banter about living the single life when behind her appeared Colin.

I must've telegraphed my surprise, because Carrie's expression told me all I needed to know. It said we're back together now, so all that "fuck Colin" stuff I said last time, let's pretend it didn't happen, okay?

So I poured the beers and I kept my mouth shut, and to my knowledge, Carrie and Colin lived happily ever after.

—

Fairy tales don't always come true, though. My co-worker Robby's sister Britney went through the most heinous breakup story I've ever heard, and she shared it with me over a few beers one night after we closed.

Britney said she'd broken up with her long-time boyfriend Matthew, and I offered my condolences.

"He was cheating on me," she professed.

Now, this kind of surprised me. She'd brought this guy around once or twice, and he was no catch. Wasting words on physical description would be irrelevant; suffice it to say he owned a lot of wide-leg Carhartts.

"That's awful," I said. "I'm so sorry."

Britney leaned forward. "You want to know the worst part? He cheated on me with a 60-year-old man from India."

I pride myself on being pretty quick with a comeback, but that sentence left me speechless.

Britney said she'd fallen into a depression after losing her job, so to satisfy his manly needs, Matthew turned to the company of internet porn. Each night he'd lock himself in his room and log on, Venmoing his hard-earned cash to cam girls for a little individual attention.

What happened next is a little hard to wrap my head around, only because I could never imagine myself committing such an act. Matthew, in the throes of internet passion, sent a picture of what Britney described as his "tiny wee-wee" to one of the performers.

I hope whatever pleasure he got from that moment was worth it, because the next day, a man emailed him a copy of this file, saying unless Matthew would like his junk sent to every address in his contact list, he should wire $500 to an account in India.

Normally, this is where the story would end. Faced with a choice of extortion or mortification, the dick-pic'ed victim would contact the police, explain what's what, and pray for their discretion.

But not ol' Matt. He paid the 500 bucks, and continued to pay it once a week for four months.

Fast forward to August, when an extra 2k a month started to get hard to find. Matthew was borrowing money from friends, falling behind on his rent, and otherwise losing his shit.

At the end of his rope, he decided to come clean to his girlfriend, who'd begun to notice the sleepless nights and thousand yard stares.

He did it in the best way possible — by getting down on a knee and proposing. He told Britney he wanted to marry her, but he had something he needed to confess first.

Britney said she was obviously taken aback and needed some time to give her decision, but after a couple of days, she went to him and said she was willing to forgive him. Yes, she would marry him, internet pimps be damned.

"Hold on," I interrupted. "I thought you broke up with him."

"I said we broke up," she said. "Once I told him yes, we could get married, HE broke up with ME."

I told her it sounded like he expected her to dump his ass and give him an out, and when she forgave him, he had no choice but to end it.

I told Britney if there's one thing I've learned from watching people's relationships, it's that love doesn't always travel in a straight line. Sometimes you think you've found the one and share that love in a handicap stall, drunk on imperial stouts. Other times you end up single because Mr. Right got blackmailed by a foreign internet porn ring. To each his own, I say.

FAMILY FRIENDLY

The sign on the front door says brewery, and based on the number of beers I pour each shift, that name tracks.

But on Saturday afternoons, you might mistake it for a Chuck E. Cheese.

There's no giant mouse — unless you count the ones feasting in the Dumpster — but everything else is on brand. Multicolored blankets spread on the floor, enough toys to fill Santa's sled, and of course, a pack of knee-high humans wreaking havoc.

I've got nothing against kids. I've got three of my own. But sometimes, when I look out at a sea of bare-chested and shoeless children, shrieking and scaling barstools, I pray for them to topple over.

I'm not rooting for permanent injuries — I'm not a monster — but a little kiss from the concrete floor would probably knock that shit right off.

—

At a playground, there's usually a sign listing rules. No running, No horseplay. At the bar, there's only one: don't let the kids drink.

Which like, fair. If you're only going to have one rule, I guess that should be it.

But as a result, all other guidelines are left to the unspoken social contract we agree to when venturing out into the world. Obvious things like don't let your child run behind the bar; don't let your child pull all the toilet paper off the roll; don't let your child wander into the production area and claw at the bucket of sodium hydroxide.

The problem when all other guidelines equate to "don't be a dick," is that people will ALWAYS be dicks. There's too much room for interpretation there. Is your kid being a dick when he sings Itsy Bitsy Spider at the top of his lungs while missing his mouth with every third Cheeto and grinding them into a fine orange powder on the floor? Is he being a dick when he and three co-conspirators turn the water fountain area into Typhoon Lagoon? Really, who's to say?

—

I can almost empathize with the indifferent parents, the ones who admonish their child building a pyramid of empty glasses in front of the exit with the deadpan enthusiasm of Willy Wonka. Stop, don't, come back. Parenting is a slog, and sometimes you just don't have the energy to give a shit.

What gets me are the enablers. I've watched parents not only endorse full-contact games on a crowded Saturday afternoon; I've watched parents organize them.

"Ok you guys, the way this game works is that whoever is holding this empty soda bottle has to keep it no matter what," I heard a guy in his mid-30s tell a gaggle of six-year-olds cartwheeling on Pepsi. "And everyone else who doesn't have the bottle, your jobs are to try and get the bottle from the person who has it." He repeated the last line like a referee in a cage match. "NO MATTER WHAT."

And that's what the kids did for the next hour, clawing and screaming like feral cats battling for the last scrap of tuna. The game only ended because the soda-bottle holder, a boy much taller than the rest, banged his head on the corner of a table and began to bawl.

"This seems like a good place to hit pause and have halftime," the ineffective dad/referee said. And the kids returned to their table to gorge on more sugar.

—

There are some craft beer purists who think kids should be banned from breweries altogether. I don't agree with an all-out ban. We're not talking about bringing kids to a brothel or opium den, but the beer nerds do have a point. Lots of people come to my bar to get away from their kids, and there's nothing more aggravating than trying to enjoy a pint in the midst of a rousing game of grade-school freeze tag.

The tricky part is trying to strike balance between being family-friendly without veering into Mickey Mouse Clubhouse. Where's the line?

Some places try to just be up front. An Ohio brewery hosts a weekly "Wu-Tang Wednesday," and it posts the following disclaimer around the taproom:

DEAR PARENTS AND PRUDES:
We will be playing unedited hip hop all day today for Wu-Tang Wednesday. Due to the nature of the music, there may be language which may offend you or your kids. Unless, of course, you take parenting advice from Ol' Dirty Bastard, in which case - WU-TANG IS FOR THE CHILDREN

One local brewery tries to find middle ground by plopping down a few picnic tables in the corner and labelling it the "family area." This is a great idea, though the space is admittedly underutilized by families due to the fact it also happens to be where they hung the dartboards. Nothing says family-friendliness like the promise of puncture wounds.

—

What's most interesting to me are the families so oblivious to their surroundings they decide the bar would be the perfect venue for their children's parties. I've seen all number of these events, including an end-of-season celebration for a youth soccer team.

This group took up three long tables: one for the parents, one for the food, and one for the kids. After demolishing a dozen pizzas that mostly ended up on the table and floor, these kids practiced penalty kicks against the taproom wall while their parents drank beers in the corner.

When I told them they couldn't play ball inside, they used a customer's Volkswagen as a goal instead. Forty minutes later, one of the soccer dads approached the bar.

"Hi, we're with the soccer team?" he said, as though I hadn't already fashioned a mental Voodoo doll out of his likeness. "One of the girls accidentally kicked the soccer ball onto the roof."

"Oh no," I said, hoping I'd sufficiently masked my pleasure.

"We were wondering if you had access to the roof so you could go and get it for us?"

I didn't have to lie to the guy, because I absolutely did NOT have access to the roof, but even if I did, I suspect my answer would have been the same. "Sorry," I said.

"Do you know somebody who does?" he said. "Can you call someone?" This must have been a really important soccer ball.

I thought for a moment about which one of my managers I could call that wouldn't hang up laughing. The answer was none. "I'm really sorry," I said. "So so sorry."

That was the end of the parking lot soccer game, but not the end of the party. The now ball-less soccer players had to get more creative with their entertainment. And they did, seeing who could jump the highest over chains enclosing the patio until we closed.

—

The absentee parents are also the ones who never want to leave. I can't tell you how many tables of drunk parents I've had to shoo out at the end of the night, oblivious to the fact we stopped serving almost an hour ago and their kids are so tired they're are melting into the floor.

One time, a foursome of mid-30s parents stayed until well after we locked the doors. The moms were so excited, repeating "we shut down the bar, I can't believe we shut down the bar," to each other, as if they were watching the sun rise over the Vegas strip and not in a suburban brewery at 10:30 on a Thursday.

The dads were equally as out of it, engrossed in a deep conversation about rifle scopes. "I just want to have a scope that can snap-drop an asshole at 500 meters," one dad said to his friends. You know, normal bar conversation.

The two little ones, who should've been in bed an hour ago, ran through the empty taproom, screeching like chimps on PCP.

When we get a table of lingerers, the bartenders try to employ subtle, passive-aggressive hints it's time to hit the road. We bring up the lights, turn off the TVs. One bartender plays "So Long, Farewell" from The Sound of Music.

I just start cleaning around them, sweeping and rolling out the yellow mop bucket. When you're trying to clear a room, the smell of Pine-Sol works wonders.

But these particular families were so engrossed in their own awesomeness, they didn't notice my co-worker, Kristen, and I up to our elbows in suds.

The kids did, though.

"Excuse me," the 6-year-old girl said to me while I wiped down the tables. "There are a LOT of leaves on the ground. Especially under our table."

"There sure are," I said, thinking and as soon as your parents take you home, I can sweep them up.

"I'm just saying, this place is really dirty," the girl replied. I thanked her for the tip and resumed cleaning, but the little girl was not satisfied.

"Are you a janitor?" she asked Kristen.

Kristen laughed. "Oh no, I'm a bartender. But we all need to do our part to clean up."

The girl considered this for a moment. "You're a JANITOR," she said. "You're a BAD JANITOR."

She and her sister then chanted "Janitor, janitor, you're a bad janitor" at Kristen while she mopped. Their parents, meanwhile, droned on.

—

The obvious thing to do when children terrorize the taproom would be to say something to the parents, but usually, I'm too chicken to speak up. But there was one party I really enjoyed ruining.

It was a Friday afternoon in June, and the happy hour crowd was filling the place up quickly. My manager told me we had a graduation party booked for the corner tables, and a couple began loading in all the trimmings: balloons and streamers and a banner reading CONGRATULATIONS SHERRI CLASS OF 2020.

We host all sorts of celebrations, so a graduation was nothing new. But then the guests began to arrive.

They were high school students. MY high school students. Sherri, the guest of honor, had been in my 11th grade English class the year before.

I don't know exactly why Sherri decided to hold her grad party at a brewery, but upon seeing me, it was clear her plans of crushing a few cold ones with her BFFs were, well, crushed.

"Mr. Hedenberg?" Sherri said as she and her friends approached the bar to order.

"Hey there everybody, congratulations on graduating!" I said. "What are we drinking?" We've got Coke, diet Coke, Sprite…"

The kids glumly took their sodas to their table, cursing their old teacher for thwarting their fun. It didn't take long for them to leave, no doubt heading to chug Mike's Hard Lemonade in the basement of a parent whose stance on drinking was if you're going to do it, I'd rather you do it in the house.

—

The thing I'd wished to see for years finally came true one Saturday around dinner time. A boy with a blond sheep dog haircut who'd been terrorizing guests for hours climbed a stool, and I watched it topple over like a Jenga tower.

It wasn't nearly as fulfilling as I thought it'd be. In fact, it was kind of horrifying. He wailed like an animal caught in a trap when he hit the concrete, and I sprinted across the room to where he was tangled in the metal barstool.

I arrived at the same time as the mom, who'd been drinking a beer with her back to him. "Is he okay?" I asked. "I saw him fall."

"Was he sitting on the stool?" she asked, or was he —"

"He was climbing it," I said.

"Oh, good. So he wasn't that far off the ground."

Real glass-half-full, Mom.

"Do you want an ice pack or something?" I asked.

"No, I think he's okay." She examined the boy's head and face. "Oh, his nose is bleeding."

"Let me get you a wet paper towel," I said.

"That'd be great," she said. "While you're at it, could you also bring me another beer?"

HULA HOOPS

A woman came in to the bar tonight with a half-dozen hula hoops slung on her shoulder. I'd love to hear the thought process that went into that choice. *Let's see, we've got the diaper bag, the snacks, a jacket if it gets chilly. Oh! And of course these six multi-colored hula hoops so the kids can entertain themselves while we pound high-gravity IPAs and ignore them.*

Have you ever been to a bar, Susan? Look at your surroundings. Do you see a lot of kids doing hula competitions? Did the bar your parents took you to when you were a kid have a limbo pole? A slip and slide? A cotton candy station? Or did you mistakenly think your nephew's 6th birthday was at a brewery?

I became further horrified when the hula hoops were distributed, not to the children running feral between the barstools, but to the adults.

It's embarrassing enough to watch uncoordinated minors trying to keep a plastic ring around their waist, but drunk adults waggling their hips and giggling is criminal.

MAN'S WORST FRIEND

When my wife and I found out we were going to have a baby, we discussed how we'd tell our kids they'd soon have a new brother.

Parents love juicing up big news. Think about how many videos you see online of kids losing their shit when they find out they're going to Disney World.

So Melinda and I sat the kids on the couch, had them close their eyes, and placed infant onesies in their laps.

Our 7-year-old daughter Josephine squealed with delight, but at 10, our son Dominic had to play it cool.

"That's okay I guess," he said. "At least we're not getting a dog."

And frankly, I agree with him. Having a dog seems like more trouble than it's worth.

Pet ownership is a tough and often touchy subject for me to talk about, because I'm under this strange delusion that dogs aren't people. I know this is not a popular opinion to hold, especially among a strong percentage of my bar patrons, who parade their pups in and out of the taproom like they're taking their niece out to dinner.

I recently served a girl in black-framed glasses wearing a sweatshirt that read Dogs are my favorite kind of people.

I'm sorry, what? Did you skip a few biology classes when you were a kid?

—

I grew up with a series of Labrador Retrievers with a collie named Rusty thrown in there. My family offered these dogs what I thought was adequate care: we'd feed them, make sure their water was full,

51

take them to the vet. They had their own fenced-in pen in the back yard and a plywood house with a corrugated roof we'd fill twice a year with straw and cedar chips. Once a month, it was my job to pick up their shit with a shovel, and on really cold winter nights, we'd let them sleep under the kitchen table.

I loved my dogs, and they loved me. When I was four and my first dog, Fred, lay on the back porch, his sides heaving his final breaths, I hid inside when my dad came out with his .45 to put him down. I helped dig the hole next to the shed several years later when Rusty died, affixing to his grave a cross made from 1"x3"s and a Sharpie marker.

This was my experience with being a dog owner. But when I share these fond memories with customers at the bar, I'm met with wide-eyed disbelief.

"You made your dog sleep outside?" one regular gasped.

"Where else would he sleep?" I said.

The customer looked down at the mound of fur at his feet and sighed. "Bella here sleeps right in bed next to me. We spoon."

"Where does your wife sleep?" I asked.

"Oh, she sleeps there too. Bella lies between us and we both cuddle her all night. It's so wonderful."

Behavior like that is hard for me to comprehend. I remember the first time I accompanied my then-girlfriend walking her dog in DC. She took a plastic bag out of her pocket and bent toward the mess the pup had just made.

"Jesus, what are you doing?" I cried.

"Picking up his poop," she said with chilling nonchalance.

I still get that same feeling when I see someone picking up after their dog. You want a companion so bad that you're willing to pick up its shit with your hands?

—

I've lived in the suburbs for a decade now, so I wasn't totally ignorant to the level of pampering owners extended to their dogs. But it wasn't until the local government relaxed health codes regarding dogs in breweries that I realized how normal it all is.

For years, we had this one guy who would come in with some dog the size of a Guinea pig tucked into his jacket. The first time I saw her little head peek out from his collar, I said something.

"Sorry man, you can't have a dog in here," I said. "It's a health code violation."

"She's a service dog," he said.

I looked the customer up and down. He'd ordered from the menu, so he wasn't blind, and he didn't appear to be missing any limbs. And since this dog couldn't weigh more than a Big Mac, I had a hard time she was opening doors or fetching the mail for her owner. I smelled bullshit.

"What, uh…what service is she providing exactly?"

The man's voice cracked. "Emotional support!"

I get that makes me look like a monster, but I really don't care what people do with their lives. If draping a boa constrictor around your neck gives you the courage to get out of bed in the morning, go nuts. All I wanted was to make sure the health department wasn't going to shut the bar down on my watch.

"Do you have any, like, paperwork that says she's a registered service dog?" I asked.

This was also the wrong thing to say.

"By law, I am not required to show you any documentation," he spat at me. "As a matter of fact, it's actually against the law for you to ask me."

I apologized and bought the guy a beer because I felt like an asshole, a feeling that dissipated quickly when I got home and learned neither state law nor the Americans with Disabilities Act covered emotional support dogs.

—

By the time I saw the guy and his pint-sized support system at the bar again, the issue was moot, because the health department updated their codes to allow establishments to be pet friendly if they so chose. My dog-loving management was overjoyed, stocking up on water dishes and biscuits that same week.

And that's when I started working at a dog park.

People came out of the woodwork with these things. Every other customer through the door was dragging — or being dragged by — one, two, three furry friends. I can't count the number of shifts I've worked where the dogs outnumber the humans, which is unfortunate because the dogs don't tip nearly as well.

One night, a guy with a Mike Brady perm sat down clutching a

Chihuahua under his arm. I poured him a beer, and when I handed back his credit card, he asked me if we had any treats.

"Treats?" I said. "Isn't the beer enough of a treat for you?"

He laughed. "Sorry, I meant do you have DOG treats."

I brought over the jar of biscuits, and the guy fed one to his Taco Bell dog. "Say thank you to the man," he cooed in the dog's giant ear. "Come on, say thank you."

When the dog just stared at me, Mike Brady apologized. "Sorry, he's being shy right now."

I told him it was okay, and I wasn't offended by his dog's lack of manners. I moved to serve another customer, and I heard him admonish the dog. "That wasn't very nice," he said. "When someone gives you a treat, you should say 'thank you.'"

This was very confusing to me, because did the dude actually EXPECT his dog to respond? If that fucking fur ball opened his mouth and said thank you, I would've thrown my rag down and walked out. Once you feed a talking dog, what's left?

———

Inviting dogs into the bar presented a number of additional scenarios I was not prepared for. I was dumbfounded, for example, by the amount dogs shed. These fuckers drop enough hair for me to construct a new dog out of the sweepings at the end of the night.

Then there's the barking. You get one overzealous pup who starts yapping at another one, and pretty soon it sounds like the pound scene from Lady and the Tramp.

When the law first changed, I thought I'd be cleaning up a lot more piss and shit, but it's really not that frequent. Usually, the owner will be so embarrassed, she'll ask for the mop to do it herself, which I decline. "I don't mind," I say, and I swipe the yellow puddle away with enough Pine Sol to drown a small village.

———

As with children, it's rarely the dogs I have beef with, but their owners. A girl wearing a shirt with a bedazzled rainbow on it must've forgotten she had her Golden Retriever tied to her stool, because after blathering with her friend and getting progressively drunk, she didn't notice the lake forming beneath her.

I stared at the piss for an hour, wondering when she would notice.

Finally, as she got up to leave, she looked down and said, "oh, shit." She scanned for witnesses the way a guilty driver does when they dent someone's car on the street, and then she dropped three napkins into the hula-hoop sized puddle.

As she yanked the dog toward the door, I thanked her for coming, and she turned back and said "I think my dog might have peed on the floor. Sorry about that!"

I've only had to ask one owner to leave because of their unruly dog, and it was one of the most heartbreaking things I've ever had to do.

The woman was in a wheelchair, and her husband was clearly not flush with brain cells. I got a lump in my throat when I watched him lift her out of her chair and onto one of the barstools, and when he asked me what he should order, I wanted to hug him.

The dog was just a puppy and also cute, but it was clear from the outset the couple couldn't control him. He barked at anyone who came within 20 feet of their table, that hostile, high-pitched yap of a young dog trying to establish its territory.

Rose, the other bartender, went over and asked the couple nicely if they could subdue the little rascal, but despite their best efforts, he continued.

"Your turn," Rose said.

Fuck. I hate confrontation so much, and I'll put up with a lot, but the noise this squeak toy made was too much.

"I'm so sorry to do this," I said to them. "But if your dog doesn't quiet down, I have to ask you guys to take him outside."

The guy with nothing between his ears apologized profusely, and he left to take the dog home while his wife finished her beer.

I felt so bad I comped one of his beers for him, and he seemed happy.

"That broke my heart," I said to Rose when they left. "they're just so cute."

"I know, but that dog was a pain in the ass," Rose said.

—

When it comes to pet owners, I've found it's best to keep my opinions to myself. I'll smile and feign interest, because to do anything else would trigger some serious hate.

Which is why I was so horrified the night I tripped over a dog on the patio. It wasn't totally my fault. The dog was black and laying on the black pavement and the sun had already gone down. I didn't realize he was there until I heard his yelp of pain.

My initial reaction was to be annoyed, because this dog was splayed across the walkway. But I also realized expecting people to keep their animals at bay was a losing cause.

So I pretended I'd just stepped on a baby.

"Can we be friends now?" I asked the pup as he took the treat from me.

"I think you're still friends," the owner replied, and I breathed a sigh of relief. I was safe from the dog people for another day.

THE PEST

We're taught from a young age the importance of individuality, that we're all little snowflakes in a blizzard, bumping together and sharing our uniqueness with each other.

And I guess that's true to an extent, but after a few years of working behind the bar, you can't help but notice a few patterns emerge.

There's basically only 10 character archetypes I serve, and once you get through those 10, you serve them over and over again.

There's the beer nerd with the neck beard who wants to talk about the flavor notes of some obscure New Zealand hop strain, not really because he's passionate about it, but to flex his encyclopedic knowledge of useless trivia.

There's the bored wife with the glass of water who's paying dearly for dragging her husband to the winery last week; the confused first-timer suavely ordering a gin and tonic; the quiet barfly who comes in every day but never says more than hello and goodbye.

Of all the stock characters inhabiting my own little Truman Show, there's one that bugs me the most: The Pest.

—

The Pest is an expert in one skill: annoying the fuck out of anyone with a pulse.

It's hard to spot a Pest right off the bat because they come in many shapes and sizes. I've met attractive young female Pests, dorky aloof Pests, and grizzled old man Pests.

The Pest is likewise an equal-opportunity annoyer. Unlike the Flirty Old Man character, who preys primarily on young female customers he wouldn't have a chance with even if he had Bradley Cooper's jawline and Jeff Bezos' bank balance, The Pest attacks with no pattern, like a shitty serial killer.

I recently had a Pest on my hands one slow Saturday night, when an afternoon storm drove the crowds home early.

I knew something was a little off when she began firing off her order without taking her eyes off the menu.

"I'm sorry," I said. "Are you ordering right now, or are you just reading the menu out loud?"

The Pest then took her beer and began what would prove to be a five-hour tour of every table in the bar.

She started outside with a group of young dorks, all of whom ordered the same tangerine saison and were chatting about their IT jobs.

"What kind of computers do y'all use?" The Pest asked. "I have a Dell, but I've heard really good things about those HPs."

It didn't take long for the guys to reach their fill of her mindless babble, and since they were too polite to ask her to piss off, they finished their beers and left, presumably to reconvene at another Pest-less bar.

This Pest even got her hooks in Frank, a regular with whom I spent 10 minutes exchanging desperate glances and a series of sympathetic eyebrow lifts.

I have no idea what she was talking to Frank about, but it was clear all Frank wanted to do was watch the hockey game.

"Can you turn it up?" the Pest called to me.

"Turn what up?" I said.

"The radio," she said. "Can you turn the radio up?"

I complied with her request by bumping the sound system's volume one notch. Which was apparently enough, because she put her arm around Frank's neck and began to sing along to the Queen song.

When she departed to use the restroom, I congratulated Frank on his new friend.

He let out a groan. "You gotta do something about her," he said.

"What do you want me to do, throw her out? Her only crime is being irritating."

"When you turned the music up, she started digging her fingers into my neck," he said. He pulled aside his t-shirt, revealing four red marks.

—

There's another variation of the Pest that's equally dangerous: The Last Man Standing.

These are the ones who come in with a large party but are having such a good time they decide to stay even after all their friends have left.

One night a group of dudes came in to celebrate a co-worker's retirement. They ran up the bill and filtered out as the night wore on, until by 7:30, there was only one guy left. He was a ginger wearing the t-shirt of a snobby brewery, the kind that serves their beer in wine glasses.

I didn't identify him as a Last Man Standing at first, because once he waved goodbye to his final remaining colleagues, he came up to close his tab.

As I handed over his receipt, he asked for a t-shirt and another beer. I poured it and gave him the total, but he wasn't understanding he needed to pay again for the new things he'd just ordered.

"Just put it on my tab," he said.

I explained he'd executed the steps backwards, that he'd closed his tab and THEN ordered new items.

He set his jaw and leaned over the bar. "I'm not trying to cheat you," he said.

"I didn't say you were," I said. "You just need to pay again, that's all."

An hour later, he was still here, wandering around and talking with strangers until they'd have enough and leave.

He even cornered a guy at a table reading a book by himself. "I love all kinds of books," he blabbered. "You put a book in front of me and I'll read it."

"Uh huh," said the reader.

I thought I was rid of him at last call, when he left his half-drunk beer on the bar. But a few minutes later he was back, this time pestering ME.

"I have a question about a customer," he said. "Do you know Reggie?"

"Doesn't sound familiar," I said.

"Big guy with a beard. Fucked up teeth. Came in here almost every night for years."

"I've worked here for awhile, and I don't know any regulars named

Reggie," I said.

"He died last year," he said.

"That's a shame."

"Yeah. I thought you'd want to know."

IN THE CLUB

Roger, one of the regulars, closed out his tab one night by handing me a $20 bill and asking for change. When I started to give him ones, he pushed them back.

"Just two fives is fine," he said. "I don't need the ones."

"You sure?" I said. "You're not going to The Moon tonight?"

The Moon is the local strip club, a sad, suburban shithole where the dancers wear pasties over their nipples. The place stays in business because it's the only strip club in a 30 mile radius.

"Dude, FUCK that place," Roger said. "The girls there are pushy bitches."

I was just kidding about the dollar bills, the way a bartender will joke about sports teams and bars and strip clubs. But Roger clearly had strong feelings about the joint.

"What's your beef with Paper Sun?" I asked.

"Are you kidding? Any place that charges $60 for a lap dance is a joke," he said. "And the girls there are bitches."

"That's the second time you said that," I said.

"It's the type of spot you gotta put the girls in their place," he said. "I tip well. I make sure I tip all the dancers, and if I like one, I'll ask them over for a drink. But when they start pushing me around, you know what I say?"

I said I didn't but I had a feeling he was going to tell me anyway.

"I say 'I know how to act in a club.' Because they have to know that I know how to act in a club, you know? I'm no amateur. I go to lots of strip clubs, so these girls need to know that. That's why I say it. 'I know how to act in the club.'"

"And that works?" I said. "You say that, and they leave you alone?"

"That's what I say the first time," Roger said. I could now tell he was drunk by the way he swayed. "After that, if they keep bugging me, I tell them to step the fuck off."

"You say that?" I said. "You tell them to step the fuck off?"

"That's right," Roger said. "I tell them 'look, I know how to act in the club. Step the fuck off.' And usually they leave you alone after that."

I thanked him for his advice, as though it was something weighing heavily on my mind.

"No problem," Roger said. "Don't let those bitches push you around. Don't forget that you're the customer. You're the one in charge."

NO MÀS

One night during a shift, a customer approached me and leaned in. "A number 13," he said. "And also, the guy behind me is passed out at his table."

I looked over his shoulder, and sure enough, there was a customer with his head in his arms. I recognized him as someone I'd served in the past, a Hispanic guy in his mid-40s with the big, rough hands of a laborer. Next to him was a younger Hispanic man who stared at his phone, either unaware or unfazed that his friend was lying unconscious next to him.

I'd only served the pair one beer each, but they'd been here when my shift started, so there was no telling how deep they were.

I filled a glass with water and sat down at the stool next to the sleeping man. "My friend, are you okay?" I asked.

He picked his head off of the table, wiping a string of drool from his lips.

"Yeah, sorry," he said. "I drank too much."

"Happens to the best of us," I said. I offered him the water, and he took greedy gulps of it.

His buddy looked up from his phone. "Two more please," he said.

Every job includes a number of unpleasant possible scenarios you pray you'll never have to deal with. At the bar, having to cut people off is the task I dread most.

Aside from possessing a strong aversion to conflict, I hate babysitting grown adults. If you're old enough to hold down a job and afford $7 pints of craft beer, you should have enough maturity to make sound choices about your alcohol intake.

Sadly, that is not always the case. I once refused service to Thomas Thomas, whose name I only remember because I thought it was ridiculous his parents named him Thomas Thomas.

Tom was in his late 30s and the guest of honor at some sort of celebration. His buddies had bought him rounds all night, and by last call he was so drunk he clung to the bar like he was on a ship in a hurricane.

Tom pointed at the menu and mumbled a sentence that sounded more like Klingon than English.

"I think you're good on beer tonight," I said. "Have a water. On me."

The man made a smacking noise with his lips and grunted. "Sorry I can't talk," he said. "I'm drunk."

"It's all good," I said. "You just need to take it easy,"

"You don't understand. I had twins almost nine months ago, and I never get to leave the house anymore."

"I can't believe you had twins nine months ago and look like that," I said. "You should be proud of how quickly you got your figure back."

Thomas Thomas giggled. "I like you," he said.

—

While giving customers like Thomas Thomas the axe is awkward, it doesn't bother me so much because at least they have an exit strategy. Most of the younger customers who are really going for it call an Uber, and other smarter ones catch a ride home with friends.

There's a small number, though, who will sit at the bar all day and then try to drive themselves home. I don't want to pigeonhole any particular demographic as culprits of drunk driving, so let's call these morons Old White Men.

Some states have laws that hold bartenders liable for over serving customers. Virginia doesn't, but the staff and I see it as an ethical obligation to keep customers safe. This makes for some truly uncomfortable situations.

A group of Old White Men held court for five hours once on a Thursday afternoon. They all paced themselves responsibly except for poor Bob, who thought he was in some some sort of one-man beer drinking contest.

Bob was in the bathroom contemplating his life choices when the rest of his crew packed up and left. When he returned, he was very confused to find himself alone.

He tried to close his tab, which he'd already done an hour before, and when he finally found the exit, he took a wide, unstable arc to his car.

"I'm going after him," Rose said. "He can't drive like that."

"I'm coming too," Vinny said.

They convinced Bob to lie down in the back seat of his car and sleep it off, but five minutes later, we watched from the window as he climbed into the driver's seat and tried to start the car.

Vinny sprinted out and again talked him into the back seat.

The process repeated three more times, until finally Bob sat on the hood of his car, staring at the pavement.

"I just ordered him an Uber from my phone," Vinny said. "I hope he lives close, or all the money I'm making tonight is gonna go toward getting him home."

—

Unfortunately, it doesn't always go that smoothly. One time an Old White Man named Jim fell asleep outside the bathroom, and when Rose offered to call him a cab, he got up and left.

Since Rose had chased down an Old White Man when we worked together earlier in the week, it was my turn to go after this one.

I followed him to the parking lot, and when he saw me behind him, he broke into a run.

You've got to be fucking kidding me.

"Hey!" I yelled. "Let me get you a cab!"

I begrudgingly gave chase, but Jim was a lot more spry than his physique suggested. He zig-zagged between cars like a child, dipping into the darkness of a broken streetlamp.

I didn't see him again until the headlights of his car flashed at the other side of the lot, and he zoomed off.

I was so embarrassed that I'd just raced a drunk old man through a parking lot — and lost — that when I returned to the bar, I lied to Rose about what happened.

I invented this story about trying to stop him, that I told him it was a bad idea to drive and even though I offered to get him an Uber, he'd politely refused.

"It's not your fault," Rose said. "At least you tried."

The funny thing is that two days later, Jim walked through the door and ordered a beer from me as though we hadn't played tag in the parking lot. Maybe he didn't remember, but I've served him at least a dozen times since, and it's never come up.

—

Back to mi hermano and his peer pressuring friend. The older guy finished his water and left a big tip, apologizing. A car pulled up and he stepped into it.

This was all fine, except for the fact he'd left his young companion sitting at the table alone.

Sensing his opening, he approached the bar.

"One more," he said.

Once you cut somebody off, they're done for the night. It's like the manager coming out to the mound and pulling a pitcher — Hit the showers, partner. You'll get 'em again next time.

"Sorry," I said. "You can't have any more."

He knitted his brow and strung a few words together that didn't quite make sense. His English wasn't great, and I could tell he was frustrated he couldn't adequately plead his case.

"I'm sorry man," I repeated. "No más."

The kid sat at his table and sulked, and though I avoided him by busying myself with other customers, I could feel him boring holes into me.

I went into the back to change a keg, I returned to find him at it again, this time harassing my co-worker Kristen.

I stood behind the kid and got Kristen's attention, making a slicing motion across my throat.

"Sorry," she said. "I can't serve you."

The poor kid sat there for FOUR hours. Every 10 minutes, he'd come up to the bar and try to order again.

"Come on man," he said after three hours of pleading and three hours of me handing him Sprites and waters. "At Hooters, no problem. Here? Problem."

"Go to fuckin' Hooters then!" I said. The bartenders are better looking there anyway."

At last call he finally got the hint. He brought a six pack to the counter and smiled sheepishly.

"There we go!" I said. "Yes, you can buy this."

A car pulled up, he walked out, and I locked the door behind him, satisfied I'd kept the streets safe for another night.

WEREWOLVES

My mom was a high school teacher for more than 40 years, and every once in awhile, she'd come home from work complaining about how her students were acting crazier than usual.

"It's because it's a full moon," she'd say. "They're always assholes when it's a full moon."

I was a kid and didn't understand anything about the moon's gravitational pull or whatever science-y stuff that might support this theory. But I did know about werewolves, so I always pictured a classroom full of them, howling and hanging from the light fixtures.

It's like that sometimes, though, when you have days where the vibe just feels a little off.

It happened to me one shift during the winter, when for some reason, every customer in the place lost their minds.

—

It started entertainingly enough with a foursome who was already pretty far in the bag when it sat down. They were older than me, I think, or at least the two girls looked more road-worn than they should've been for mid-30s.

One of the girls kept talking to me, but I couldn't hear her, partially because she was whispering and partially because she was slurring.

On the sixth time of "I'm so sorry, could you say that again," I got "blahblahblah Hawkeyes," and I used my superior bartending skills to infer she was asking me the score of the Iowa football game.

I told her I didn't know, but I could look it up if she wanted.

"Csdflkjalk Iowa," she said, which I took to mean she was from

Iowa.

"I love Iowa," I said. "It's a great place."

"People get FUUUUCKED UP in Iowa!" she yelled, suddenly finding her voice. "Like, really fucked up!"

"I think that happens in a lot of places," I said.

We went back and forth for a minute more about how she loved Iowa, me agreeing over and over. And then she said:

"Y'wanna know the best thing about Iowa?"

"Sure."

"All the girls there got big TITTIES!" Then she cupped her boobs and jiggled them at me.

"Now I feel weird, so I'm going to walk away," I said.

I was a little uncomfortable, yeah, but mostly I didn't want to disagree with her. I've met plenty of Iowa girls with small boobs.

——

Even after my Iowa customers peeled themselves from their stools and went home, things stayed weird. A girl in her mid-20s, who'd been sitting with her parents and boyfriend, left her table and began dancing in the middle of the floor. The song was Kansas's "Carry On, My Wayward Son," and right as the chorus hit, she began twerking against a trash can.

My co-worker Vinny and I thought it was great, and we spent the next 20 minutes manipulating her through song: Journey, Bon Jovi, Billy Joel.

"Dang," Vinny said. "I wish I was on her level."

As I wiped off the bar, she stood in front of me and started dancing seductively to "Sweet Caroline."

"Impressive," I said, because what else do you say to a girl grinding to Neil Diamond?

"It's just for you," she said, then sauntered away.

It was clear she was really feeling herself, because then she walked over to another table of younger customers and started talking shit.

"I noticed your man was looking at my ass," the girl said. "It's probably because you ain't got one."

Thankfully the other customers didn't take the bait, and her parents finally collected her and closed their tab.

"Weird night," I said to Vinny.

"Weird night," he replied.

We only had an hour until last call, but it was just getting started.

—

Not long after the classic rock twerker had departed, I was in the back filling the mop bucket when Vinny stuck his head around the corner and asked if I knew the non-emergency number to the police department.

He explained one customer was trashed, and as he stumbled to his car, some Good Samaritan customer — also trashed, by the way — tried to stop him.

She was probably mid-30s, wearing a Jane Fonda pantsuit and no bra. She had this guy, late-40s in a Dickies worksheet with the name of his auto repair shop embroidered over the breast pocket, backed into a corner and was talking to him awkwardly.

"Should I just call 911?" Vinny asked.

"Hell no!" I said. "I don't think you should call at all."

Vinny sighed. "I'm gonna call."

I manned the bar while Vinny went outside to use his phone, and every few minutes drunk pantsuit lady would look at me with impatience.

"Why aren't the police here?" she yelled. "They need to get here NOW."

"I'm sure they're on their way," I deadpanned, abandoning all hope of getting home at a decent hour.

"Call 911!" she urged.

"Ma'am, 911 is for emergencies. Do you feel like this is an emergency? Are you or this man in danger?"

"Well no, but…"

"Then I'm sorry. We'll just have to wait until they get here."

The cops did finally show up, a young redhead with a sleeve of tattoos and an older guy wearing a bored, sleepy expression.

"Is he causing a disturbance?" the ginger cop asked. "You want us to arrest him?"

"He hasn't really done anything, honestly," Vinny said. "We just didn't want him driving home like that."

The ginger cop frowned and the older cop yawned. "Unless you want us to lock him up for the night, there's really nothing we can do," he said.

They managed to get the dude out to the curb, where they tried to talk him out of getting into his truck. They called a cab for him, but once the cabdriver saw the guy's condition, he screeched off like the cop just asked him to take home Ted Bundy.

Eventually, they took him home themselves, even though they tried like hell to avoid it.

—

After the cops left, the drunk lady in the Jane Fonda pantsuit recounted her harrowing experience to every remaining customer.

She ran the customers out table by table until she found herself alone. Then she turned her sights on Vinny and me.

When her Uber pulled up, she came and held out her arms like we were long-lost friends. "Thanks for everything," she said.

I took a step back. "I'm pretty sweaty," I said, but she came in anyway, getting her no-bra grossness on me.

"It's okay," she said in my ear. "I sweat too."

I watched her pull away, thankful to be finally done with the night, and as I looked up, I saw it.

It was a full moon.

86

Something my non-bartender friends always ask me about is how I handle the rowdy customers. They must imagine each of my shifts is like a scene from *Roadhouse,* where I spend time between pouring pints hip-tossing customers out the door.

The truth is far less exciting. Since we close early and don't serve liquor, most customers behave themselves, which saves me a lot of grief.

The closest I've seen to a fight between customers was when an old-timer gave a group of soldiers hell for drinking in uniform. There was some finger pointing and a brief scuffle, but cooler heads prevailed and everyone went their separate ways.

—

In the five years I've worked at the bar, I've only had to throw one customer out. And it was a doozie.

My partner Marty and I were getting ready to close up for the night, and there was this one guy still standing at the bar waiting for his ride. *Leaning on it,* might be a more appropriate description. He was in his mid-40s and wore a dirty NASCAR hat over a mop of greasy curls.

The guy started talking to Marty's wife Melissa, who was waiting for us to finish up. If he was flirting, he was doing a piss poor job of it.

"What's a pretty girl doing sitting here all alone at the end of the night?" he slurred. "Are these guys taking care of you or what?"

Marty overheard the guy's advance and told him jokingly he took care of her just fine. "You see that ring?" Marty said.

The guy scoffed. "If you take such good care of her, how come I seen her in here shaking her ass all night like a whore?"

I swallowed a laugh because Melissa hadn't moved from her stool in an hour, but Marty didn't think it was funny. He slammed his palm on the bar. "Get the fuck out!" he said.

The guy puffed his chest and set his jaw. "You gonna make me?"

"Okay, okay, we're good here," I said. Both Marty and the customer were bigger than me, and I wasn't interested in breaking up a brawl. I took Marty by the shoulders and led him into the back to cool off. "I'll handle it," I said.

I tried to be as polite as possible. "I'm so glad you came by tonight, I said to the guy. "But I think it's time to go."

"I wasn't talking to you," he said, craning his neck around me to try and spot Marty. "Mind your own business, pussy."

I'm allergic to all forms of confrontation, but getting called a pussy raised my ire.

I pulled my lips into a smug grin. "I hope you have a great night, sir."

"You want me to go?" he said. "Come make me."

I smiled wider. "I don't think you understand," I said. "I *am* making you. We'll see you next time, okay?"

Just as the guy leaned over the bar to grab me, the door opened. It was his friend, there to pick him up. He sized up the situation quickly and took the guy by the arm. "I'm really sorry," the friend said. "He does this sometimes."

The guy yelled obscenities over his shoulder on the way out the door. "Toodleoo!" I replied, waggling my fingers at him. "Drive safe, now."

I turned to Melissa, who'd been quietly watching the scene unfold. "See what happens when you come in here and shake your ass all night?" I said.

—

While the drunk NASCAR fan was the only customer I've ever had to kick out, I did also once have to 86 a trivia host in the middle of a game.

Trivia Thursdays were one of our busiest nights, and our usual host was a plump fellow with an Amish beard who looked a lot like the harmonica guy from Blues Traveler. But on this night, it was a substitute host, a girl in her late 20s who wore a scowl from the moment she walked in the door.

Attitude aside, the poor woman was not built to host. She mumbled through questions and mispronounced key words. Even with the microphone to her lips, her voice came out just above a whisper.

It only took about 15 minutes for the packed bar to start complaining. "Speak up!" one yelled. "We can't hear you in the back," shouted another. After she pronounced the Brazilian city *Ry Day Janier,* one man began to boo.

And that's when she snapped.

"Listen, you motherfuckers wanna come up here and do it yourself?"

The bar fell into silence. It was the clearest thing she'd said all night.

"You don't like what I'm doing, then fuckin' leave."

The other bartender and I looked at each other. "Oh, shit," I said.

The crowd started to turn on her, half of them grumbling in shock, others in offense. Several tables packed up their things and left.

Unless I wanted an empty bar, I needed to say something.

"Hey-yy," I said to the host in a singsongy voice, aware the entire room had their eyes on me. "Is everything okay?"

The girl hurled a string of insults, her head shaking from side to side. "Nobody's going to talk to me like that. This is bullshit."

"I'm awfully sorry about that," I said. "But would you mind not cursing at the customers and telling them to leave? I'm trying to run a business."

She began pointing over my shoulder, cursing at a table of customers. "What the fuck are YOU looking at?" she said.

"I think it would be best for everyone if you just pack up and go," I said.

She glared at me for a moment, doing the math to see if smacking the smug look off my face would be worth it. She sucked her teeth and grabbed her laptop. "Fuck this and fuck you," she snarled.

The bar erupted into applause as she broke down her equipment, and for the rest of the night, customers offered me high fives and praise. "That was AWESOME!" one guy told me. "I thought she was going to hit you!"

It might not make the list of all-time bar brawls, but for that night, I was a hero of *Roadhouse* proportions.

TO THE VIDEO TAPE!

When I was little, my friend Bill's mom owned a restaurant, and sometimes, we'd hang out there while she worked.

My favorite part was sitting in the office and watching the security monitor, a grainy black and white TV that showed a live view of the restaurant.

We never saw anything more scandalous than a server lick a knife after she cut a piece of cake, but it still thrilled me to watch someone without them knowing. I felt like a spy.

That's why I was so excited when I discovered the brewery had a camera mounted over the bar, and you could watch it from the office computer. The security software was called Blue Iris, which sounds like either the name of a dystopian overlord or a rapper's daughter.

—

I found some functional uses for the security cam. If I was accused of half-assing cleanup at the end of the night, I'd tell my manager to check the tape.

Most of the time, though, the other bartenders and I used Blue Iris for entertainment. Whenever something funny would happen during a shift, I'd write down the time it occurred. Then, once we were done for the night, we'd pour ourselves a beer and review the daily hilarity. "To the video tape!" we'd yell.

I saw some great things on that camera. Like the time a keg exploded on me, drenching me in beer. Or when a guy with no legs was pulled off his stool by his charging dog and dragged across the floor.

For awhile, a few of us were convinced two of our colleagues were hooking up, even though they denied it. So every time that pair worked together, we'd pull the footage and analyze every frame for flirtation like it was the Zapruder film.

—

The leading role in our hidden camera show was played by Gene, our owner.

Gene was an affable egghead who wanted so bad to be a part of the cool crowd. He earned his MBA from Harvard after he was discharged from the Navy, and he paired his wide-leg dad jeans with checkerboard Vans slip-ons.

Over the years, Gene and I developed a great relationship. When my family visited me at work, he'd drop everything and sit with them, playing games with the kids and telling Melinda how much he valued having me as a part of the team.

Gene LOVED to mingle with the customers, introducing himself as the owner, or, as he put it, "the poor son-of-a-bitch in debt." He'd schmooze with a table for a bit and then comp them a few drinks. He relished that clout.

He always meant well, but dealing with him while behind the bar was annoying. When Gene was in benevolent owner mode, he tended to treat us poorly, talking down to us and making demands. We'd be deep in the weeds and he'd cut the line and tell us to pour him a round. "When you get a second," he'd say, which translated to drop what you're doing and get me this now.

We also resented the number of beers he comped. When he was rolling, he'd hand out one or two to every table, which significantly cut into our tips.

"Looks like Gene's sticking around tonight," Marty would say to me.

"Awesome," I'd reply. "Do you think it'd be easier for me to just hand him the tip jar now?"

—

Gene always started his work day at 8 a.m. by pouring himself a beer and sitting at the bar with his laptop. That's a long day to be drinking high-gravity IPAs, so every once in awhile, Gene would miscalculate his beer intake and get a little too loose.

I've already talked about how serious the staff and I took over-serving customers. We always had their best interests in mind, and if we started to get nervous about it, we'd cut someone off, even if it made for an awkward conversation.

But how do you tell the sweet guy who signs your paychecks that he's had enough?

Unable to muster the courage to confront him, we did what any uncomfortable staff would do:

We mocked him mercilessly behind his back.

We'd watch as he teetered from table to table, reciting his same son-of-a-bitch in debt spiel to anyone who'd listen. After we closed, we'd review the security video, laughing at him missing the table when he tried to put down his glass or putting his arm around a nervous customer. Nights when Gene put on a show always provided incredible prime time footage.

—

During my third year at the bar, Gene went through a nasty divorce, something I wouldn't wish upon my worst enemies.

It was heartbreaking. We all knew he was hurting, but he wouldn't talk about it. He kept everything bottled up, I think, because he didn't want his personal shit dragging down the business.

The problem was, Gene compensated by spending more and more time at the bar, lingering until last call. Those accidental nights of getting a little too tipsy became more common. Gene transformed into The Pest.

The bartenders didn't really care because it just provided us with more fodder for our nightly screenings. Gene getting touchy with a woman while her husband looked on. Gene falling into a four top. Gene having intense conversations with a couple too polite to send him away.

His target of choice became young females. When they came in the door, he'd pounce like an overzealous car salesman, pushing free drinks at them and bragging about this being his place.

It became so frequent, we started placing bets on how long it would take for him to approach single ladies once they sat down.

"I'm setting the over-under at four minutes," I said when two blonde college-aged girls entered on a Wednesday night.

"Five bucks on the under," Marty said. "That's a sure thing."

He was right. Ninety seconds after they'd ordered, we watched Gene as he locked on with his T-2000 vision and sauntered over. "Hey there," he said. "First time here? I'm Gene, the poor son-of-a-bitch in debt that owns this place."

"He shoots, he scores!" Marty said, and I forked over a five.

—

One morning at the beginning of our shift, Marty came in the door, his eyes wide.

"Dude, you're never going to believe this," he said. "The night crew told me Gene was in here last night after hours. WITH TWO STRIPPERS."

We had an entire taproom to set up before the doors opened, but this couldn't wait. "To the video tape! I yelled, and we scrambled to the office.

Sure as shit, there was Gene, stumbling in the door three hours after we closed with two girls dressed like extras in a Cardi B video. Marty and I clutched each other and giggled as we watched him pour them drinks and gesticulate wildly.

"How in the world did he pull this off?" I said.

"I mean, they're not exactly first stringers," Marty said.

"But is this what he's doing at night? Recruiting strippers to come with him so he can show off his bar?"

Marty shook his head. "Dude's a fucking mess," he said.

"An entertaining mess," I said. "This shit is gold."

About a week later, Gene came in at 8 a.m. like he normally did. He poured himself an IPA and sat at the bar. When his glass was empty, he walked out the door.

Then he went home and took his own life.

—

I was teaching a grammar lesson to my English class when I found out. The air left my lungs.

Gene is dead.

I barely made it home because I had this intense fear that I was going to crash and die. I found myself consumed with guilt; not because I felt like I could've done something, but because of the way

I'd made him the butt of my jokes.

In order to make sense of the world, we put people in these boxes. At the bar, I do it all the time. There's the Feng Shui Artist, the Discount Seeker, the Absentee Parent, the Pest. The Hilarious Drunk Boss.

When I watched Gene on those tapes, laughing at his behavior, that's all he was to me; a flat character on a screen. I chose not to see that his antics might have been indicative of something much bigger.

—

The day after Gene died, Marty and I found ourselves behind the bar again. Neither of us felt very good about it. We were still fighting our own demons and not looking forward to the deluge of questions we knew we'd face.

What happened?

He passed away suddenly.

How?

He passed away suddenly.

Marty and I didn't talk the whole shift. At the end of the night, we each poured a beer and looked at each other. This was when we'd normally watch the day's security footage. But both of us knew what was waiting for us if we fired up Blue Iris: the last images of Gene, the poor son-of-a-bitch in debt, sitting alone at his dream bar, drinking his last earthly pint.

Tears welled in Marty's eyes, then mine.

"To Gene," he said, and we clinked our glasses together.

I never looked at the security camera again.

ACKNOWLEDGEMENTS

Writing a book is hard, and I'm grateful to have people in my life who've supported me through my many false starts and bad ideas.

First and foremost, a huge thank you to my colleagues, many of whom served as my first audience as I told these stories during our shifts together. Charlie, Chris, Matt, Jack, Alvin, Alycia, Greg, Hibah, Kerry, Garrett, Colin, Clea, Caitlin, Max, Potsy, Jackie, Nico, Wes, Ryan, and anyone else I spent time in the weeds with over the years.

To Casey, a guy I miss every single day.

Likewise, a thanks to the customers who've shared their problems and joys with me over a pint or four.

To The Prompt writers, especially Kelaine and Josh, who are forever my cheerleaders and publish whatever I word vomit onto the page.

To Dominic and Josephine and Robert, who give me a reason to keep going.

And most importantly, thanks to my wife Melinda, who works endlessly so I have time to write, who puts up with being portrayed as a nag in every story, and who tells me after every draft — no matter how shitty — "eh, it's pretty good."

ABOUT THE AUTHOR

Sam Hedenberg is the author of *The Endless Bummer: In Search of the Perfect Family Vacation* and the humor blog IDontBelongHere.net. He's a frequent contributor to The Prompt literary magazine. He lives in Northern Virginia with his wife and three children.

Made in the USA
Monee, IL
28 November 2021

82844263R00056